Life Compass for Women

The Indispensable Guidebook on Life Management for Busy Women

Connie L. Aden • Karen L. Anderson • Lillian Zarzar • Larna Anderson Beebe
Heidi Richards • Paula Baum • Allison Blankenship • Marilyn J. Amendt
Toni Boyles • Susan Concannon • Ann E. Mah • Susan Meyer-Miller
Connie Michaelis • Debra Neal • Jae Pierce-Baba • Vicki Trembly • Darla Arni

COMPASS
SERIES PUBLISHING

For information contact:
Compass Series Publishing
3351 SE Meadowview Dr.
Topeka, KS 66605-3022
1-785-266-9434
Email: ann@CompassSeries.com
Web: www.CompassSeries.com

ISBN # 0-9754076-0-0
FIRST EDITION

Quality Compass Series Publishing^{SM} **Books:**

Life Compass for Women:
The Indispensable Guidebook on Life Management for Busy Women

Career Compass for Women:
The Indispensable Guidebook for Women in the Workplace

TABLE OF CONTENTS

TABLE OF CONTENTS

INTRODUCTION

Life Compass for Women is about women helping women succeed in life. It was written for you by members of the American Business Women's Association who are also professional speakers, trainers, and authors. Whether you are a stay-at-home mom or the CEO of your own company, life management is an issue with which we all struggle. We are *all* busy women. This book provides a compass for life success and strategies you can put to work today.

Each chapter is a mini-workshop full of thought-provoking ideas to help you take stock of your life direction. Don't feel that you have to read this book from front to back. Just choose the topic that intrigues you most and start there. Some chapters are just plain fun and others challenge you to dig deep for greater meaning in your life.

Life Compass follows a long tradition of education for women. When Hilary Bufton, Jr., founded the American Business Women's Association in 1949, the purpose was to bring together women of diverse backgrounds to learn business skills. In the early years, the members broke new ground by simply daring to meet together in the evenings!

Now we break new ground again by sharing our expertise on everyday life situations with women everywhere. We have included contact information for each co-author on the first page of her chapter. Most co-authors provide additional services and can be reached through their websites. At the back of the book, you will find listings of other resources available from the co-authors including books, tapes, and programs.

I hope you find *Life Compass* enjoyable as well as helpful. In it we share our stories and tips for successful living the same way that women have always shared their stories.

The Best of Success to You!

Ann E. Mah

Ann E. Mah
Co-Author and Editor
Owner – Compass Series Publishing
ABWA 2002 National President

PS: For information about ABWA, visit www.abwa.org
PPS: For information about the complete *Compass Series*, visit www.CompassSeries.com

CHAPTER ONE

In Pursuit of NOWability

Connie L. Aden

A little package with a powerful punch might be the best way to describe Connie. Her messages hit you where you live. They are, at the same time, warm, funny, impacting, genuine and based on her extensive experience as a wife and mother, a coach, a corporate and nonprofit executive, a board member, and an entrepreneur.

After a successful career in the telecommunications industry, Connie parlayed her knowledge into a thriving fourteen-year-old consulting business. Her specialties are human resources, customer care, diversity, personal effectiveness and smart business practices for small and medium-sized companies.

Volunteer positions have also added to Connie's experience and knowledge, from serving as the National President of the American Business Women's Association to chairing the board of one of the largest credit unions in the country.

She authored two training manuals on diversity for the National Credit Union Association. Connie also wrote and appeared as the lead facilitator in a nationally-marketed diversity training video. Her workshops on coaching, customer care and management development draw rave reviews from participants.

Being at the point in her career where she can pick and choose her projects, Connie only does what she is inspired to do and she loves every minute of it. Training and public speaking are two of those inspirations.

Aden Management Resource
Green Valley, AZ • 520-393-1373 • adencl@msn.com

Connie L. Aden

In Pursuit of NOWability

Life, we learn too late, is in the living,
in the tissue of every day and hour.
– Stephen Leacock

Freeze your thoughts! How aware are you of where you are, with whom you're speaking, and what's going on around you … or is your thinking in another place and time?

Consider the idea that many of us ignore or don't take the time to simply ponder. In our lifetime there are only three places we can live … the past, the future or the NOW. Where do you spend most of your time? Is where you live getting in the way of your participation in a happy and productive life?

Many of us spend the majority of our time in the past or the future, even though these are the two least satisfying and productive places to live. We have all heard the adage stop and smell the roses, which is just another way of saying slow down, see what's around you, pay attention, stop living in the past or the future and start living in the NOW.

Do you get caught up in the should-haves of the past or the what-ifs and as-soon-as traps of the future? Do you find that you can't focus on and live an authentic life in the NOW because the choices and decisions you made in the past keep pulling you backward? Are you always delaying the things you want to do by telling yourself that you will do them "as-soon-as"? Have you put your life on hold until: The kids leave home? You get a better paying job? You get your social security? You have more time available? Or any one of a number of excuses we have all used at one time or another?

NOWability is developing the habit of focusing on and living in the present ... the NOW.

NOWability does not require that we forget the past or the lessons we learned from it or that we not anticipate and plan for the future. It does require that we relish each minute, hour and day that we have right here and right now. It is about focusing all of our attention and energy on the events and people in front of us. It is also about interacting with others on a "right here, I'm present" basis. It calls for intensely listening to under-stand the real meaning of what is being communicated to us. It requires that we savor every one of our senses as we go from minute to minute in our lives.

NOWability means that we don't get caught up in letting the past or the future paralyze us into indecision and inaction. How often do we let our mind focus on should-haves and what-ifs and as-soon-as's? When we fixate on these scenarios in our lives, we risk missing much of the living of it.

So ... where are you living your life? The following exercise will help you start the thinking process about where you are expending most of your time and focus.

Respond to these scenarios by answering:

Usually, Frequently, Occasionally or Never

— After a conversation, you can't remember some or all of what was discussed.
— Many of your decisions are delayed until something else happens.
— You have difficulty concentrating on current problems because ac-tions or decisions from the past still need to be resolved.
— You feel guilty because of things you did or did not do in the past.
— You let possible problems or roadblocks derail you from making decisions.
— You drive to an appointment and have no idea of what you saw along the way.

This list is just a teaser to get you thinking about where your focus and mind-set are as you live each minute of your life. If you answered Usually or Frequently to most of the questions, you probably live much of your life in the past or the future and very little of it enjoying the NOW.

What, you might ask, can you do to live more in the present? Let me share a true experience of one young lady when she realized that much of how she lived her present life was dictated by her past.

SARAH

Sarah is a young wife and mother in her mid-thirties. Sarah felt stuck in the past as a result of actions taken and decisions made after graduating from college. She also felt a sense of guilt about the things she had not done according to expectations, either her own or those of others. She said these concerns were sucking away her energy and getting in the way of her being able to focus her thoughts, time and energy on her current life. For example, she had completed her course work for a master's degree, but after five years could not seem to get her final thesis completed. She worked on it in bits and pieces, requested extensions and fully intended to get it done. It consumed her thinking. When she was playing with her children, she worried that she should have been working on her paper. When she applied for jobs and wrote her resume, she was concerned that she had to explain why she hadn't actually received her degree. Her thesis was at the back of her consciousness at all times.

Perhaps you have a similar story … something that has nagged at you for years. Once Sarah decided that she had had enough and was ready to do something about all that past baggage, we put the following process in place to help her return to the present. Consider if this process will work for you.

RECLAIMING YOUR NOW LIFE

1. Make a list of all the things you think you should have done, the things that pop up and nag at you, the things that make you feel less than you are, and the issues that still are not resolved in your mind. Stay open. Free-flow with your list. Don't make any judgments about what should or should not be included.

    (Examples from Sarah's experience … completing her master's thesis, upgrading her conversational skills in French and Spanish, getting a teaching certificate, pursuing her interest in professional photography, corresponding with a friend in France, apologizing for something said that hurt another person and even sending a photograph promised several years before.)

2. Review each item by asking yourself these questions. Why does this still have relevance to me? Is there anything that I can or will do to correct this? How important is it in my current life? Why do I feel I have to do something about this situation? Will it make my present life easier if I take action now?

3. Identify those items on the list that no longer have relevance, those that you can comfortably disregard and those you choose to no longer care about. Put these items on a separate list and on that page write yourself a note that gives you permission to dismiss them, forget them and drop them from your worry inventory. Put this sheet in a secret place and if one of the items comes up again, review the note to yourself and let it go again ... or destroy the list and symbolically purge those concerns from your life. *(Sarah tells me this technique really works.)*

4. The remaining items become part of your action plan. Prioritize each item by the amount of time required to resolve the issue and ease of completion. (Give yourself a break and some early successes by completing some of the simpler items first.) Take each concern and identify positive steps you intend to take to complete the task and remove it from your worry list. Be specific and detailed. Set time lines and identify resources. *(Sarah chose a simple task as her first accomplishment—that of sending the photograph. It required that she find the slide, have it made into a photograph and write a letter of apology. For her most complex task of completing her thesis, Sarah put the following plan together. She identified time lines to meet the university's deadline. She recruited resources to help with her children and give her uninterrupted time for research and writing. She devised a strict schedule to complete a certain amount of work each day. Finally, Sarah sought out experts to review and critique her work and give her advice.)*

5. Work your plan. Be practical and patient. Don't be afraid to ask for the help that you need. Don't overwhelm yourself by trying to accomplish everything on your list in the first two days. Be realistic about what you can accomplish and make sure that you spend time each day advancing your plan.

By the simple fact that you have faced and acknowledged the concerns of the past, you have started to take back your present. As you work your plan, you are living in the NOW … and once each of your concerns is marked on your list as "accomplished," you will discover a new energy to relish and cherish the current world around you.

> *You have got to own your days and live them,*
> *each one of them, every one of them,*
> *or else the years go by and none of them belong to you.*
> – Herb Gardner

For those of us who spend much of our time in the future dealing with the "what-ifs" and the "as-soon-as's," activating our NOWability habit can be a real challenge. Let's review the following situation of a woman who lives almost entirely in the future.

CARRIE

Carrie is 45 years old, recently divorced and has an eleven-year-old daughter. Carrie survived a negative relationship in her marriage and says she is ready to move on with her life. She wants male companionship and some fun, but nothing is happening to move her closer to that goal. Money is tight and she is fearful about the security of her job. When I asked Carrie about her situation, this is what I heard: As soon as I lose some weight, I'll start looking for ways to meet men. What if I lose my job and have to sell my house? What if the divorce scars my daughter? As soon as I'm secure in my job, I'll have some extra money and can take my daughter on a real vacation.

All of these concerns are valid issues. However, procrastinating on making decisions or taking action does nothing to help the situation. Living in the future means that opportunities in the NOW are being ignored, overlooked or dismissed and the joy of life is diminished.

We used a couple of very simple techniques with Carrie, similar to that used with Sarah.

For the "what-if" issues:

- Carrie made a list of all the fears, worries, concerns and possible disasters she could imagine in her life.

- For each item on her list, she developed a contingency plan of what she would do if that event occurred. Her plans were specific and detailed.

- She kept her plans in an accessible place so she could refer to them easily. If other items bother her in the future, they can be added to the list and addressed in the same way.

"What-ifs" are our fears. They get in the way of our enjoyment of today. They limit our vision of the possible, bog us down and keep us from taking action to make things better. By identifying those issues and knowing exactly what we are going to do if they happen, we no longer have to think about them. We take away the worry and anxiety (because we have a plan) and replace it with the ability to focus on the present, which is the habit of NOWability. If you live a future-oriented life, perhaps you will find this technique helpful when you start the "what-if" whirlwind.

Nothing in life is to be feared.
It is only to be understood.
– Marie Curie

For the "as-soon-as" issues:

No one wants you to give up your dreams. What we want is to take charge of those dreams and move them progressively closer to reality. The "as-soon-as" statements are our way of expressing our vision of what we want from our lives and how we think things should be. However, wishing and dreaming don't usually get us what we want. They remove us from the real world of today and keep us from enjoying what is right in front of us. The solution is to keep our dreams and do what we can each day to move them closer to fulfillment.

In Carrie's case, she decided she could put aside a dollar a week toward that vacation with her daughter, cut out advertisements from the newspaper and magazines about places they are interested in visiting, and go to the local library to do research on the Internet or through travel books. Carrie also realized she doesn't need to put her interest in finding male companionship on hold until she loses weight. She can do both at the same time. She started a healthy eating routine, along with a walk each day and a simple exercise program. She began identifying places where she might find someone with compatible interests, e.g., her daughter's softball games, local parks with sports facilities, her church, single-parent groups or classes at the community college.

The solution to dealing with "as-soon-as" issues is to take small steps toward the reality of it. To do what you can here and now to make your wish or dream come true at some future point … that is NOWability.

The difference between the techniques I've suggested to you and others you might have encountered in the past is understanding how to stay on track and not just making another "to do" list. This is your authentic life plan. The difference is about focus and making a commitment to a NOW life. Most of the time we operate on "automatic pilot." We let our habits carry us through the day. We don't think about our thinking. In order to develop NOWability we have to change our existing habits and become more mindful of the place we're living in and what thoughts are driving us.

IMPORTANT STEPS TO
DEVELOPING THE NOWability HABIT

- Recognize what it is you want to change: the should-haves, what-ifs and as-soon-as statements. You have done that if you have completed the previous exercises.

- Identify the steps that will accomplish the change you want to make. Your detailed plan is your roadmap.

- Post your roadmap in a prominent place and work on some piece of it daily.

- Make a commitment to yourself to concentrate on where you are, who is speaking to you and what is happening around you at all times … in other words, *FOCUS*.

- Journal your daily NOWability successes and those occasions when you weren't so successful. In this way you will know how ingrained your new habit has become and what adjustments need to be made in your thinking.

- Finally, but most important of all, be gentle with yourself. As with any habit, you have to keep practicing it daily until it becomes harder to do the old than it is to do the new.

REMEMBER...

The most important thing in our lives
is what we are doing now.

– Anonymous

We all have times in our lives when it is difficult to stay centered in the present—when events of the past or concerns of the future pull us away from the NOW. The good news is that you have choices and control over how you handle those times. When you live your life in the present, you participate in the fullness of life. Therefore, test the methods I have suggested. Start with something small. Trust in your intuition, judgment and decision-making ability. Develop an ongoing process of looking at your current habits and replacing the ineffective ones with those that focus on the NOW. I know you will experience capabilities beyond your expectations once you have a little help getting started. Consider the information provided in this chapter as the nudge you need to begin taking back the NOW.

Good luck as you begin your journey ... in pursuit of NOWability.

CHAPTER TWO

The Band Is Playing. Are You Marching?

Marilyn J. Amendt

A former Iowa farm wife who became a New York senior vice president, Marilyn's story is one of inspiration to working women everywhere. She raised three sons and used her talents, drive, and determination to become an expert in human resources. She is a much sought after corporate executive, often referred to as the "idea woman."

Marilyn worked twenty years in human resource management, establishing executive training programs as well as being an ex-. ecutive in-house consultant. She serves as keynote speaker, seminar facilitator and actively works with companies to recognize and develop their biggest asset—people.

She is a past national president of the American Business Women's Association. Marilyn has also served as Board President for the Young Women's Resource Center in Des Moines, Iowa. She is recognized in *Marquis Who's Who of American Women*, *Who's Who Among Human Resource Professionals,* and *Who's Who in Professional and Executive Women*. Marilyn is a Presidential Director with the National Companies and is president of her own company, Success Strategies.

Even though others would be thinking of retirement, Marilyn shows no signs of slowing down. Her chapter teaches us the secrets of continuing to grow and learn.

Marilyn J. Amendt
Des Moines, IA • 800-307-8323

Marilyn J. Amendt

The Band Is Playing. Are You Marching?

Do you remember the first time you saw a parade? Maybe you helped decorate a float or marched in a band. Did you feel the excitement and enthusiasm of the crowds? As a clarinet player, I loved being a part of our high school band, marching proudly, wearing my uniform and contributing to the music.

Did you ever notice a band marches on even when the music has stopped? Watch the Macy's Thanksgiving parade sometime. Marching is action—it's "go"—it's momentum. If you were ever involved in a parade, you knew you were an important part of the action and vital to the celebration of the festivities.

Although high school was fun, it was in college that I got turned on to life. New beginnings can be frightening, exhilarating, and beneficial because they can lead to achievement. When you left home for the first time, what was the hardest thing for you? Was it being with people you didn't know or perhaps learning a new method of doing things?

I experienced all of the above in college. I was away from home, lived with a stranger called a roommate and attended classes three times larger than in my high school. That's when I said,

WOW! This is different and new.

Some people call this "growing up." You are constantly being exposed to new and different situations.

Janie, in her first year of college, said she felt overwhelmed. She was a good student in high school, active in sports, busy socially and was anxious for college, but she said she was numb for the first month trying to put it all together. Eventually she adjusted and felt college was a normal way of life. She described it as, "A learning experience everyday. My mind opened up to new ideas," she explained, "testing new strategies of thought, questioning my professors, and trying some of these new ideas or perceptions on my friends and parents."

These wonderful years of ages 17 to 25 can be called the "explorative stage." You believe you know the answer to life's questions and are frustrated that adults seem so unbelievably ignorant. The explorative state is exciting and full of discovery. You are in eager anticipation.

From the age of 30 to 50 we are more focused on gaining a financial edge. Our concerns tend to be job status and building personal relationships. Our friends and family say we are settling down.

A very successful businessman told me that people really don't know much until they reach age 50. I questioned him on this statement. At the time, I was in my 40s and believed I knew quite a bit. He said it is all the choices we make between 30 and 50, the mistakes from those choices, or the rewards we reap, that give us the knowledge to be successful and build our character. And, since I've reached my 50s, I have found wisdom in his statement.

The following exercise will help you define the significant factors that have added to your personal growth:

1. The people I have met. (Was it a mentor, parent or associate?)

    _____

    _____

2. The jobs I have held. (List in importance to your learning.)

    _____

    _____

3. The risks I have taken. (Those that taught you the most.)

    _____

    _____

4. The education I have had. (Include college, on the job, and continuing education courses.)

    _____

    _____

5. The relationships that have meant the most. (Those that feed your heart and mind.)

    _____

    _____

As you review your answers to the above questions, you may realize you had forgotten the significance of them. Each factor is a steppingstone on your path of personal growth. Can you visualize how much you have grown personally? Look at the many resources available to build your character as you start each new day.

What in heaven's name is so great about retiring?

Eventually life progresses and we are faced with retirement concerns. When I looked up "retire" in the dictionary I read: to withdraw or retreat. What a dismal view of life. Who would want to withdraw from or pedal backwards in her life?

If you believe current advertising, the goal for people is to "retire early" or "plan now to retire." You start to think withdrawing is life's goal. WRONG!

Life's goal is to keep on living as healthy and happy as you can—not to retreat!

The key is to embrace life's experiences, set goals continuously, and work toward them. Don't send me any "happy retirement" cards. Instead, congratulate me on my latest achievements.

What if medical science stopped looking for breakthroughs and said there is nothing you can do for people when they reach 60, 70, 80 or 90 — just let them retreat from life and die. What would life be like? Sadly, I see people who give themselves license to do just that—quit!

This business of living is unfinished as long as we are breathing.

Yes, we struggle, but that struggle builds character and provides us with knowledge. Many times we find out what we are capable of through struggle.

Consider the butterfly. It must struggle in the cocoon. This struggle emits oils and fluids that give it color as well as strength. When it is time— the larvae emerges from the cocoon flying with its beautiful, new body for all to admire.

If the years 17 to 25 are the explorative stage, and 30 to 50 spent gaining our financial edge, the years 50 to 65 become the "living the life of least resistance" stage. We give up when all we really need to do is to resurrect our explorative stage attitude.

So many people stop dreaming. Too often they use the words "I can't", and we all know that once you think you can't, you are right. I became a believer in positive thinking after falling in love with Dr. Norman Vincent Peale's book *The Power of Positive Thinking*. One thing seems certain, positive thinkers are having more fun!

My friend Betsy worked in the social care field for most of her adult life. She became an outstanding executive director of a nonprofit agency for 10 years. During this time she helped the agency grow from a $50,000 annual budget to a $200,000 annual budget with sustained growth in every area. She was recognized in the community for her success and for her loyalty and commitment to the agency. But after some reflection, she decided to do what she had always wanted to do—become a nurse. At age 55 she started her college education to become an R.N., and she will soon graduate to work with senior citizens.

When have you said, I have been doing the same thing so long, I need a change. But what will I do? How can I accomplish it? What will it take?

Betsy said she had many concerns about her career change so, she wrote down in two columns the reasons for and the reasons against and evaluated those factors along with where her heart was leading her. Betsy said, "It's been a struggle for sure, but I'm personally growing so much and have such a feeling of accomplishment."

You deserve excitement and the thrill of achievement.

Making the most of your experience is like putting cash in the bank. But you first must step out and try new things, take risks, manage well and seek helpful resources. Here are some things you have to do to get more from life.

1. Embrace Change

Change is nipping at our heels every day and in numerous ways. It enhances our lives like the television, the dishwasher or cell phones. At times, change can be difficult and unwelcome when we fail to see the benefit or it demands we do something out of our comfort zone such as lose weight, give a speech or learn the computer. However, change can also be a catalyst for greater things.

Several years ago I was asked to join the American Business Women's Association (ABWA). After attending a chapter meeting, I saw businesswomen networking and learning how to advance their business skills, and I joined.

What a change for me when I had to give my first report to the chapter members. With knees shaking and voice trembling I did it—and felt good about it. My self-confidence grew to where I accepted the office of chapter president. I continued to accept more responsibilities. When the chapter members told me they wanted to nominate me for a national office, I declined. I said I was too busy, which actually meant I was scared to death. They asked me to think about it. I knew it would be a big change to try for a national office, but I wanted to try.

We put a team together and prepared for campaigning at the national convention. We won. The next year we won vice president and the following year we won president. What a change for me. I was learning so much about the value of teamwork, for it was my team that got me elected.

My professional career and personal lifestyle was enhanced because I embraced change. It was a tremendous opportunity that I nearly threw away.

Other women have shared similar stories with me of how their lives and careers were more successful because of their willingness to embrace change. Elizabeth had always wanted to be in a play. Reluctant to try out, she offered her services of costuming or painting scenery. Finally she decided to try out for a part in a play and was selected. What joy to reach her dream. At 60, Elizabeth never thought she would be good enough to do it. Now she's on stage as often as she can be—either on center stage or behind the scenes. The lessons of life's experiences are rich in helping us adapt to change. Change asks for our patience and perseverance.

2. *Set Daily, Weekly, Monthly, and Yearly Goals*

It is said that people don't plan to fail, they fail to plan. Writing down goals is an exercise of thought, desire, emotion and dreaming. It leads to your future. It stimulates the mind and aids in setting a course of action for achievement.

Write your goals clearly and concisely. Carry them with you and when you are waiting in an airport or for an appointment, look at them and read them out loud. They will make an imprint on your unconscious mind. What the mind can believe the body can achieve.

3. *Develop an "I Can" Philosophy*

This quote by Steward Johnson gives us direction for marching along life's path:

Our business in life is not to get ahead of others,
but to be ahead of ourselves—to outstrip our
yesterday by our today, to do our work with
more force than ever before.

My business career started when I became a store manager for a national retail company. Prior to that I was an Iowa farm wife for 20 years and raised three terrific sons. Faced with a change in my lifestyle and a strong need to increase my financial status, one of my goals was to own a successful retail company. My first step was to work for one that was credible with smart leadership and poised for growth. After two years as a manager I was asked to accept a position as corporate personnel director in Duluth, Minnesota. Yet I had no formal training in personnel work.

This is when the "I can" attitude kicked in. I did what many of you would do—relied on my common sense and past work experience. Day by day I learned and through support of others I became the best personnel director I could.

Start by doing what's necessary; then do what's possible,
and suddenly you are doing the impossible.

– St. Francis of Assisi

How many times have you been given the opportunity to do some task or take an office or chairmanship that you at first said to yourself, I don't have enough skill or knowledge to do that? But you really wanted to try. What usually motivates us to try is a need or a goal—or perhaps both.

How do you eat an elephant? Eat just one bite at a time and you are suddenly doing what was once the impossible. (Note: I have yet to find anyone who wants to eat an elephant!)

Eight years after moving to Duluth I accepted a position with the parent company in New York City. The parent company owned 11 retail apparel companies and I was Director of Personnel. I took a big drink of "I can" juice every morning and utilized every ounce of my positive energy to think, plan, act and do what was necessary.

I had a good handle on the job—it was all the unknowns about living in the "Big Apple" that made me anxious. Never afraid to ask questions, I soon had regular New Yorkers eager to help me learn about their fabulous city and how to survive. I loved every day of my years spent there. Walking down Fifth Avenue was very stimulating.

My "I can" attitude and positive energy was really tested. Now I know the true meaning of "If you can make it there, you can make it anywhere." Who would have thought it possible for an Iowa farm wife to succeed in New York City?

4. Be Teachable

Always keep thinking, reading, and listening. In John C. Maxwell's book *Thinking For a Change*, he writes

Everything begins with a thought. What we think determines who we are. Who we are determines what we do. Our thoughts determine our destiny.

Being teachable means being open to learning and having a thirst for knowledge. Read or listen to tapes a minimum of 20 minutes per day—choosing something to help you reach your goals. Since our thoughts determine our destiny, we need to be sure our thoughts are clear and beneficial to the lifestyle we desire.

Two of my favorite books are *The Journey From Success to Significance* by John C. Maxwell, and *Eat That Frog!* by Brian Tracy.

5. Develop a Healthy Lifestyle—In Other Words, Stay Fit

A healthy lifestyle includes eating properly, getting enough sleep, and sufficient physical exercise. Getting enough exercise seems to be hard for most of us. It takes discipline. I could find ten things to do before I would exercise on my own until I met Sara. Sara is a

successful businesswoman who believes that everyone should include fitness in her life. At age 25, after receiving her degree in
fitness, she launched her business, Priority Fitness and Body Works.
She has grown her business from in-home to her own clinic.

A personal trainer, Sara comes to my home twice a week for one
hour. Our routine includes working on flexibility, strength training and Pilates. Cardiovascular I do mostly on my own. Do make
this one of your priorities.

Gaining greater flexibility is huge for everyone. Experts tell you
this helps ward off old age. Staying fit gives you more energy and
more confidence. Another tip is to find a good massage therapist
and add that to your routine.

Who better to invest in than yourself? Every cent spent on a proper
fitness program is worthwhile. Why not do body maintenance instead of buying medicines for ills that result from neglect of a
healthy lifestyle?

6. *Persist in Spite of Obstacles*

It takes determined focus on a goal to remove obstacles. The people
who are champions in my book are those who in spite of obstacles
(health, mental, financial) worked hard to make a rewarding life
for themselves. We all encounter barriers in our lives at some time.
It is how we challenge ourselves to remove them, and how committed we are to doing whatever it takes to grow and thrive in spite
of these obstacles, that makes life fulfilling.

> **In my personal dictionary, retirement means
> pursuing another phase of life—not quitting,
> or withdrawing, or retreating.**

Achievement at any age gives new meaning to your life. All that
you have experienced, all that you have overcome, all that you have
given to others, creates new levels of ingenuity and momentum as you
march forward.

Opportunities are created when you are nurturing the seeds of "What's next?" or "What if?"

Your road needs a planned destination. It is a destination only you can determine. You have amassed many dependable resources to rely upon. Now move forward. Have joy in your heart, purpose in your mind, and keep your body moving. If the music has stopped, keep marching with the band—the melody is in you.

CHAPTER THREE

To the Keepers of the Hearth and Flame
Five criteria for GREAT relationships

Karen L. Anderson, M.A., CTD

Author and professional speaker, Karen L. Anderson investigates what makes people do what they do. She is also fascinated by how ethical, empathetic leaders influence and inspire others to do what the leader wants.

After three decades of professional and community service in roles that include being a department leader, a corporate trainer and consultant, an adjunct professor, a civil mediator, a certified trainer and developer, a construction manager, and a business owner, Karen is still baffled by human behavior. Her insights will entertain and encourage you in your pursuit of happiness and freedom of expression.

Karen's clients include the Environmental Protection Agency, the United Way, Honeywell, Meals on Wheels, Sprint, national professional associations, universities, and individuals seeking self-development. She has shared and exchanged learning with thousands of seminar participants and students.

Karen's mission in life is to help others transform communication skills into persuasive strategies for creating positive choices and connections in the world. Karen will be pleased if your world as you know it—and your relationships as you live them—improve as a result of her experiences and expertise.

Anderson Catalyst Training Services
Lenexa, KS • 913-492-3881 • www.acts-ion.com

Karen L. Anderson, M.A., CTD

To the Keepers of the Hearth and Flame
Five criteria for GREAT relationships

Coals can grow cold, warm a home, or burn blisters into our skin. How we care for those coals makes the difference. The same is true with relationships. We have all experienced turning cold, being warmed, or being burnt in relationships. Traditionally, women have kept the ancient flame of hearth and home alive by being the emotional communicators through words and deeds. Historically, a woman served her father, then her husband and her husband's children. Women accepted what was expected of them: to initiate and maintain relationships among families and neighbors. Women absorbed the anxiety around them, and they worked hard to be good caregivers, worriers, and martyrs. In return, the men provided economically and environmentally for the women.

When I attended college in the 1960-70s, my folks expected that I would meet and marry an educated man who would take care of me while I raised a family and created a home for us. Women of my generation were encouraged to become secretaries, nurses, or teachers until they married. After all, those occupations would prepare women for housekeeping and childrearing without threatening the male professions in leadership, management, and supervision.

Occasionally, a strong woman, such as my friend Geneah, evolved from this historical scenario. She once explained to me, "I choose not to worry. I'll need that energy when something really does happen." She was a dedicated public school teacher who raised three successful sons, and she used her considerable energy to deal with their bigamist father. It took her 31 years to sort it all out. My friend triumphed, saying, "I got myself into this mess, and by golly, I got myself out!" She determined never to marry again—not because she didn't trust men, but because she didn't trust herself to judge men. She made a conscious choice to be without a husband or life partner.

Although families, support networks, neighborhoods, and businesses are built through relationships, merely managing these relationships does not guarantee that they are healthy connections. Young girls, for example, spend hours concocting wedding scenarios and romantic adventures. Most of the young brides I have known, including myself at nineteen, were shocked when the reality of adulthood simply could not compete with the idealism of their daydreams! I have watched my grown children and my co-workers struggle with personal and professional relationships. Fortunately, observation and experience lead to insight. The five criteria that surface frequently regarding relationships are Growth, Reciprocity, Esteem, Authenticity, and Trust. GREAT relationships are made, not born. Reality tempers idealism in healthy relationships. Because people skills require deliberate intentions, consider the following characteristics as you evaluate your current personal and professional relationships.

1. Growth

Growth is the process of learning while striving for mutual and compatible goals. Business associates and life partners alike share visions and dreams that they want to achieve together. The core values and priorities they determine become the basis for future decisions and actions. Employees work to achieve the organization's goals. Parents schedule children's sports events into the family calendar. Whether a corporate team member or a family member, an individual may have additional objectives that healthy relationships can accommodate by planning ahead.

For instance, a mother tells her children in exasperation, "Help me find a way to say yes," when they ask for transportation to two separate social events during her scheduled business meeting. Amazingly, the children suggest solutions that had not occurred to the mother. At work a supervisor approves personal leave for a family reunion for a compatible goal or training for a technological skill set as a mutual goal. Planning and scheduling a vacation requires both the co-workers' support for compatibility and family members' support for mutuality.

Growth through goal setting plays a large role in the business arena today. Paul W. Swets identified five characteristics of effective SMART goals. He said they must be: Specific, Measurable, Affirmative, Realistic, and Time-Constricted (*The Art of Talking So That People Will Listen*). But he forgot a sixth one—Supported! The modified SMART-S model ensures both compatibility and mutuality so that effort to attain a goal is supported and not sabotaged. Partners can help each other reach their goals by removing obstacles, suggesting strategies, or encouraging persistence. My husband states proudly that he has learned he either helps me or he gets out of my way when I am focused feverishly on a mission. Whether at the office or in the home, a relationship partner can get out of the way to make a goal compatible, if not mutual. Consequently, growth creates experiences and possibilities for living a deliberate, conscious life with disciplined and informed risk—a life that is more subject to positive change than to negative chance.

2. *Reciprocity*

Another GREAT characteristic is reciprocity, as demonstrated by the following story. Chuck—hungry for lunch—waits for Betty to arrive home from running errands. Betty parks the car and hurries into the house. She says, "Honey, I'm sorry I'm late. What kind of sandwich would you like? Oh, you'll need to get gas; the gauge is on empty." Chuck replies that he knows how the car must feel because his tank is empty, too. They chuckle. Betty recalls a time when a migraine forced her to bed before lunch. Chuck brought her soup in bed. On another occasion, Chuck had retina surgery and the doctor instructed him to avoid bending. Betty drove Chuck to his doctor's appointments and maintained the car for several weeks while her husband recovered. That's reciprocity: negotiating roles, agreeing to the rules of conduct, and fulfilling expectations.

During World War II, women worked in factories and citizens rationed supplies to assist the war effort. In recent years, devastation from terrorism in Oklahoma City and New York City rocked our nation. Americans turned into a united family, committed to freedom and security, by providing immediate emergency assistance and outpourings of prayerful wishes. World leaders debate economy and peace in terms of reciprocity. A young couple sacrifices the wife's income while she studies for a professional license and the promise of greater benefits and rewards. Somewhere, someone is covering briefly for a co-worker, working overtime to complete a project on schedule. That's reciprocity in action.

Reciprocity means work and life partners have responsibilities and expected roles to perform in both anticipated and unanticipated contexts. Reciprocity reflects our sense of justice and fairness. Without reciprocity, the structure becomes less flexible. Unresolved emotions escalate. Tension swells to frustration that leads to resentment that transforms into anger that festers into rage that ignites into violence. Taking tensions and frustrations seriously as early as possible behooves us all. Conflicting expectations and roles must be identified and negotiated in healthy relationships.

3. Esteem

Esteem is how we value ourselves and others. It is influenced by our experiences and perspectives. How we use our power impacts esteem. Positional power is exercised when a police officer gives a citation. An assistant leading the annual United Way effort exercises situational power. A fundraiser having lunch with a community or corporate leader hopes to utilize political power. We witness personal power when a co-worker says, "Stop making offensive remarks in my presence. If you continue, I will file a written complaint with your manager." Clearly, how one uses power within a relationship affects the esteem of the parties.

It is widely known that many victims reside with abusers through cyclical episodes of battering. This may be because either the victim's self-esteem is poor, based on learned helplessness or because the victim experiences a shift in relational power during the apology stage of the cycle. Such a shift in power is a typical, yet unhealthy, reason to remain in a relationship.

To establish healthy esteem for yourself and others, focus on affirmations and encouragement. Begin all new relationships by accentuating your similarities with the other person. Commonalities provide the foundation for celebrating differences later. An example is showing gratitude for a team member's talent, skill, or idea, thus building esteem by adding value to the diversity within the team. Ironically, that value creates a sense of unity within the team, improving morale and esteem.

4. Authenticity

Healthy relationships provide safe environments for the fourth characteristic: authenticity. Being openly honest as one stands up for her own beliefs means a person can be herself without apology or censure. History made it difficult for Mary Ann Evans, also known as George Eliot, to be authentic as a nineteenth-century British novelist. She had to disguise her gender with a male pseudonym to have her books published and read.

Within the past thirty years, the American people have found it difficult to forgive presidents who lie to them and then deny the American public an apology. Presidents Nixon and Clinton fell into the trap, and new evidence suggests Kennedy withheld full disclosure of his private and political life as well. Authenticity issues permeate constitutional rights, civil rights, and gay rights issues. Authenticity expresses itself in face-to-face confrontations with opponents or accusers. Authenticity also expresses itself honorably and peacefully without fault, guilt, punishment, or penalty.

Authenticity is nurtured through the Six H's of Healthy Communication: Hunger, Here, Honor, Heart, Hope, and Humor.

Hunger: Until someone is hungry to know or learn, save your words.

Here: Concentrate on the present time because most of us are too busy to visit the past or the future.

Honor: Maintain dignity for you and for your relationship partner.

Heart: Show empathy and compassion. Offer words and deeds that heal rather than harm.

Hope: Encouraging statements and goodwill gestures reflect possibilities for positive change.

Humor: Smile and laugh to break the tensions in life and keep a positive perspective.

The lack of authenticity promotes gossip, infighting, and back stabbing, according to Dr. Harriet Lerner, author of *The Dance of Anger* and *The Dance of Intimacy*. She also studies how secrets and silence injure relationships. These secrets and the impending struggle to maintain silence can undermine the strongest individual and the best relationships, says Dr. Phillip McGraw, author of *Life Strategies, Relationship Rescue,* and *Self Matters*. He even suggests on his television show that losing weight is connected to being authentic. The lesson is simple, although not always easy: be authentic, speak up, and speak out. You are the best advocate you have for healthy relationships!

5. Trust

The fifth characteristic of a GREAT Relationship is trust, which encompasses credibility, rapport, and time-based experience. Credentials are what first influence people: authority, accountability, accomplishments, knowledge, resources, and reputation. Then people get to know each other and are influenced by agreeability and flexibility. Rapport develops based on how much they have in common and how much they like one another. Over time, reliability and endurance complete trust through one's personal experience with a relationship partner. If one partner in life or business receives an urgent request for help from the other, the partners know they can count on one another to be there.

Geneah experienced the abuse of trust in her marriage. Her husband was untrustworthy, but even more regrettable, Geneah distrusted herself in future relationships with men—as if she were responsible for their untrustworthiness! To trust oneself and to trust the process of life, one must choose the risk of disappointment and the blessing of forgiveness. When we misjudge another's character or fail our own standards of integrity, we become disillusioned and disappointed. Trusting our families, neighbors, clients, and colleagues factors into our relationships by adding to the quality of life. Being open to receive a "good and right and true" life is to trust one's own learning in the process of living. Perhaps it is impossible to have a trusting relationship without first trusting oneself to make healthy determinations in one's own learning, expectations, and self-concept.

Putting all five criteria into operation on a daily basis takes commitment. The following story reflects this commitment.

They have a second marriage with a blended family; no easy task for any couple. The wife quickly drove the hours of highways from Tulsa to Kansas City to arrive in time for an evening movie with her husband. Entering the house, she saw a note from her husband. He had just left with his adult children to see the very movie she had told him she wanted to see with him.

Hurt and angry (authenticity), she threw her bags down and located the newspaper for show times. Realizing she could stew or she could create possibilities (esteem), she decided to treat herself to the next show. Her husband arrived later to find a note from her saying that she was disappointed he did not wait for her and that she would be home around 11:00. That disappointment caused her to remember when she stood him up for a lunch date. Her priority had been to coach her daughter through a small crisis. He had understood. Maybe tonight he, too, had extenuating circumstances (reciprocity).

The hour before midnight, the couple took turns sharing their perspectives of the day. He had agreed to the spontaneous movie excursion with his children to accommodate their inflexible evening schedules. The husband knew he could see the movie again with his wife. He knew that she would understand (trust). After embracing, they had a lively discussion about the movie, just as they would have had they seen it together (growth).

So there you have it: how to make a GREAT Relationship! When tension or frustration arises with a relationship partner, diagnose where the symptoms occur and take action to heal the pain, quell the fear, or fulfill the desire. Your relationships will improve, and your ability to articulate your needs regarding growth, reciprocity, esteem, authenticity, and trust will increase. Keep the coals glowing in hearths at work and home that nurture healthy connections. Your quality of life depends on it!

CHAPTER FOUR

Good Fences Make Good Neighbors
A quest for conflict resolution

Larna Anderson Beebe,
M.A., DGD, BFA, DTM

Larna Anderson Beebe is an inspirational speaker, trainer, author and futurist. Her mission is to assist professionals to proactively increase passion, productivity and profitability. Born and educated in South Africa and now living in the USA, Larna offers a fresh and profound perspective on various hot topics. All presentations are made memorable through interaction, true stories and humor. She combines acute observation with working knowledge of life, science and business to stimulate audiences to map a future path.

Larna has worked as a marketing and management strategist and consultant for fourteen years, both in the corporate environment and as an entrepreneur. Larna is presently a Toastmasters International District Governor for an eight-country District. Larna is also a member of the National Speakers Association. She holds a master's degree in Marketing and Management and has earned the highest qualification awarded by Toastmasters International, the Distinguished Toastmaster Certificate.

Larna's commitment to sharing what she has learned about individual and business improvement has led to a demand for her services as a speaker and trainer. Embracing lifelong learning, Larna continues to fine-tune her medley of presentations that have been adapted to a variety of audiences and industries in nine countries.

Larna Anderson Beebe
Overland Park, KS • 913-642-1114 • www.responsegroup.com/larna

Larna Anderson Beebe, M.A., DGD, BFA, DTM

Good Fences Make Good Neighbors
A quest for conflict resolution

Good fences make good neighbors. Or do they? Robert Frost puzzled over this proverb in 1915 and built around it a thought-provoking poem. Here is an extract from *Mending Wall*:

> "Why do they make good neighbors?
> Before I built a wall I'd ask to know
> What I was walling in or walling out,
> And to whom I was like to give offence.
> Something there is that doesn't love a wall."

To avoid criticism, do nothing, say nothing, be nothing.
–Elbert Hubbard

If you are alive you will encounter conflict. From bedrooms to board-rooms to borders, conflict is inevitable. What is conflict? *Conflict is a disturbance of equilibrium caused by strong emotional reaction to real or perceived differences.* Differences build around five root causes, namely material possessions, needs, wants, principles, and perceptions. Often there exists a complex mixture of these five causes. Eyeball to eyeball disagreements can be healthy. However, when conflict begins to drain energies, gets underhanded, or threatens emotional or physical harm, it becomes something to deal with.

You can get much further with a kind word and a gun
than you can with a kind word alone.

– Al Capone

Battlefields, guns, courtrooms, walls and fences are evidence that peaceful resolution of conflict is not inevitable. What is resolution? *The process of resolution involves changing conditions or transformation.* Successful conflict resolution involves dealing with feelings in a factual way. Emotions are neither right nor wrong. The process of reaching resolution often includes hearing some surprising things that are normally safely tucked away in our blind spot. *The result of resolution is surpassing previous limitations or transcendence.* Resolution is a quest for a yin-yang balance between anarchy and dictatorship, everything and nothing or complacency and violence.

Why should you care about conflict resolution? Ignored or badly handled conflict feeds the imbalance which leads to broken relationships and reduced productivity, as well as decreased motivation and morale. Conflict handled well fosters improved relationships, increased productivity and innovation. How you handle conflict is determined by the pain-pleasure principle, your past experiences with conflict and your skill level in dealing with conflict. Expectation of benefit motivates while fear of consequences de-motivates. It is hard to remember the most appropriate way to deal with conflict when it flares in a split second. The challenge is to internalize the skills of conflict resolution so that appropriate response becomes matter-of-fact and second nature.

Point to Ponder:

What do your figurative walls and fences look like and how might your life improve if they were either reinforced or removed? As you read the next section, take a moment to jot down situations in your life that make you climb the walls and assume the on-guard fencing stance.

The number of participants in conflict can range from one to millions. Because conflicts mirror each other to various degrees, the same resolution skills and steps apply to simple or complex conflicts. The quantity and intensity of the emotions invested in the conflict determine the time the process will take. The skills required include active listening, assertive speaking and deep sixth sensory understanding. How can you use these conflict resolution skills in your daily situations?

Active listening involves showing empathy without interrupting. Nodding or phrases such as 'I see' or 'I understand' show empathy. Simple misunderstandings can be cleared up with active listening. Active listening can be remembered by the acronym EAR, which stands for Encourage, Appreciate and Review. Encourage with phrases such as "tell me more." Appreciation is expressed by saying "thank you for telling me." Review using probing words such as "do you mean …?" or "is there anything else?"

Assertive speaking requires fifty-fifty talking to ensure equal give and take. Speaking in the first person is more credible and eliminates shift of focus. An example would be to begin by saying "I have experienced …" or "I feel that …" Using second person speech, like "s/he said …" implies alliance, gossip or hearsay. Conflict resolution can be slower when dealing with people who are either unable or unwilling to articulate well, such as little children who do not have the words or those who struggle to put words to their experiences. More patience and encouragement are required to help such people get an equal share of the conversation.

Deep sixth sensory understanding is about your nonverbal communication. By letting go of ego and intellect one remains open-hearted and open-minded. This is the essence of any heart-to-heart conversation. It is the ability to perceive with all the senses rather than just mental cleverness. It is the ability to understand a unique situation, without interrupting with your own similar tale, that is appreciated. It is not appropriate to show negative emotions when listening to someone pour their heart out. Self-control is required to refrain from frowning, letting your mouth hang open or even shaking your head. Self-control is called for in order not to judge someone when they are expressing their deepest feelings.

Point to Ponder:

Everyone has a preferred strategy or instinctual style when encountering conflict. Read each of the following resolution methods twice. On the first read, reflect on a situation when you observed the response detailed. Dig deeper on the second read. Can you identify your style?

Good wishes alone will not ensure peace.
– Alfred Nobel

When Alfred Nobel's will was made known after his death in 1896, it was disclosed that he had established a special award for the promotion of peace. This was to atone for inventing explosives including dynamite. He never intended these inventions to become weapons of war.

Patterns of Prevention – Attempts to prevent conflict may have a deterrent effect but do little to teach life skills. Examples include scanners for luggage or metal detectors at airports, train stations and schools. Threats of punishment such as grounding or fines are commonly used preventative measures. It is wise to establish clear house rules for children that promise either reward or punishment. Unnecessary conflict is prevented and children learn better when all family members participate in setting boundaries and agree on the consequences of either toeing the line or crossing the line.

That old law about 'an eye for an eye' leaves everybody blind.

– Dr. Martin Luther King Jr., 1964 recipient of the Nobel Peace Prize

Determined to Deny – Doing nothing about conflict could be interpreted as cowardice or complacency. Pretending that no conflict exists will not make it go away. Unaddressed conflict usually grows. However, postponing confrontation is a good strategy when the time or place is inappropriate, when you need to calm down or need preparation time. Acknowledge the situation and schedule a specific time to deal with it. This in itself is a step toward resolution. If someone does something that bothers you, tell her. If you suspect that you have offended someone, ask her. Assure the person that it is because you care that you are mentioning the matter rather than choosing to deny it and let a more complex conflict develop.

The awareness that we are all human beings together
has become lost in war and through politics.

– Albert Schweitzer, 1952 recipient of the Nobel Peace Prize

Competing for Conquest – The conquest method is especially evident in war, business or divorce. When one party goes all out to win, he/ she may resort to aggressive strategies such as violence, shouting, bullying, cheating, threatening or manipulating. These responses are the result of failed collaboration. Refusal to come to the table is often motivated by a need to be right. Conquest is unproductive as the battle may be won but the relationship will be lost. Principles, self-esteem and the opportunity to learn are compromised. War does not determine who is right but only who is left. The challenge is to distinguish between enemies or competition and teammates or loved ones. In other words, if you value the relationship then the quest should be to join forces on the same side. Is it really "you against me" or "us against the situation?" Those who insist on one-upmanship win no friends.

> *Never insult an alligator until you've crossed the river.*
> – Cordell Hull, 1945 recipient of the Nobel Peace Prize

Dominating by Designation – This is a tactic of using authority to dominate people in lesser roles. Those pulling rank tend to solve problems by saying "because I said so." This solves nothing but adds more bricks such as resentment, embarrassment and helplessness on top of the original wall. A more thoughtful approach ensures cooperation and lasting results. Domination should only be used when a life-threatening emergency demands insistence on a particular behavior.

> *If you fear making anyone mad, then you ultimately probe*
> *for the lowest common denominator of human achievement.*
> – Jimmy Carter, 2002 recipient of the Nobel Peace Prize

Accommodate when Appropriate – Accommodation is a good tactic when an outburst stems from reaction to an unusual or temporary situation. When reaction is out-of-character, the person may just have had a stressful day. It may be enough to remind the person that you are on her side and are ready to listen when she is ready. Giving in and going along may be appropriate when a greater good exists and if the offended party can proceed without martyrdom, grudge or doubt. Obliging then becomes something you want to do rather than have to do. For instance, if your spouse arrives home with the news that his CEO just announced layoffs, to chastise him about forgetting to buy bread on the way home would be inappropriate. Accommodation is better than compromise when confronted with a known choice. For example, you may have to choose between a once-in-a-lifetime opportunity to attend a live performance of your favorite star or to attend your mother-in-law's funeral. Accommodation is a bad tactic if it creates a habit of passive or aggressive strategy for either party.

If we have no peace, it is because we have
forgotten that we belong to each other.
– Mother Teresa, 1979 recipient of the Nobel Peace Prize

Fix it Fast – A quick-fix gives the illusion that conflict has been resolved. An example is physically separating people into different classrooms or departments. When children fight over a toy, confiscating it is a fast yet temporary fix. This response is appropriate when people not directly involved in the conflict are being unnecessarily disturbed. No real progress or reconciliation takes place when the causes and emotions of conflict remain unresolved. At an appropriate time and place, the arguing parties should be brought together to arrive at a resolution.

It is not the facts which guide the conduct of men,
but their opinions about facts which may be entirely wrong.
We can only make them right by discussion.
– Sir Norman Angell, 1933 recipient of the Nobel Peace Prize

Cutting for Compromise – Compromise is workable if you are satisfied with getting only part of your needs or wants. To bargain over possessions or a price may be fun, but compromise is not a game. Compromise is not an option when differing principles are the root of the conflict. It is possible for parties to walk away with a written solution yet still feel frustrated and cheated because of concessions made. As a result, the participants may be less committed to the decision. The method of compromise calls for power sharing and excellent negotiation skills.

In the practice of tolerance, one's enemy is the best teacher.
– The 14th Dalai Lama Tenzin Gyatso,
1989 recipient of the Nobel Peace Prize

Agree to Disagree – Agreeing to disagree is appropriate when no amount of negotiation is going to budge someone from a principle or preference. Respect, tolerance and even humor prevent differences from growing into dividing walls. With the knowledge that an impasse is inevitable, debate can be healthy jousting or become tiresome. You need to be secure within yourself to gain anything from such differences.

If you want to make peace with your enemy, you have to
work with your enemy. Then he becomes your partner.
– Nelson Mandela, 1993 recipient of the Nobel Peace Prize

Cooperation for Collaboration – Collaboration is the most rewarding and lasting way to resolve conflict. Everyone wins when all parties
work together for mutual ownership of the resolution. Willingness to work
side by side turns opponents into allies. This calls for trust amid the tur-
moil of emotions. It also calls for creative thinking, accountability and
responsibility. While collaboration may take more time and effort, participants will have greater commitment to the resolution.

We cannot control the situations where conflict arises, but we can
always control how we approach the resolution. Here are five steps to
follow when faced with resolving conflict and you want to try for a col-
laborative resolution:

1. Define the boundaries – Clarify the boundary rules so that the resolution
    process begins with feelings of hope and security. Boundaries create
    attitudes and an atmosphere conducive to resolution because every point
    of agreement is progress. Some rules to agree upon may include that it is
    desirable and possible to resolve the conflict. You may also agree upfront
    that there is no such thing as a stupid emotion or question, that there will
    be no belittling or name-calling, and that sincere apology is not a sign of
    weakness. Agree to attack the problem, not the person or personality.

2. Dissect – Gather and give information regarding feelings, facts, fig-
    ures and foundations. Pooling information empowers all participants
    to contribute. How might this sound? "I feel ___ when ___ because I
    prioritize / need / want / believe / prefer ___ ." This step also serves to
    identify the exact areas of agreement or disagreement. A shared goal
    could be to maintain and improve the relationship. Differences could
    revolve around qualities or quantities.

3. Decide – Generate many creative solutions with all participants mak-
    ing suggestions. Brainstorm in a way where proposals are not evaluated
    or analyzed. Once all the suggestions are on the table, search for mu-
    tually workable solutions by objective evaluation. Decide on the best
    resolution that will benefit all participants. What might this look like?
    "I agree to ___ by ___ so that ___ ." This answers the "who, what,
    how, where, when and why" questions.

4. Reconcile – A signature, handshake or hug can seal an agreement. Even friendly resolutions can be put in writing. This serves as a reference of accountability and adds significance to the process. Written agreements should be kept by the participants rather than added to a file where they can later be taken out of context. Take action to implement the resolution. This could entail developing positive behavior or abstaining from negative behavior. Appropriate action indicates that you value the relationship, keep your promises and sincerely seek success.

5. Review – Schedule a time and place to ensure that all participants who crafted the resolution find it workable and beneficial. This reassures participants of ongoing fairness.

Collapse of Collaboration – Suppose you have approached the conflict with utmost calm and professionalism, but there still is no resolution? Consider mediation. Mediation is appropriate when negotiation reaches an impasse or fails. Neutral intervention also can be constructive when the participants are uncooperative or ill-equipped to resolve the conflict. A mediator is a trusted neutral party with good communication skills who acts as a referee. A good mediator is able to suspend judgment until s/he has heard all the facts, is a good listener, and is able to keep confidence. For example, you could serve as a mediator when your children are having a fight and cannot work things out. Your pastor can mediate for you and your spouse during a difficult time. Your human resources manager might be a good person to turn to when you have conflicts at work.

Pleasurable and positive associations are created by consistent masterful resolution of conflict. Acceptance of conflict and internalization of resolution skills as matter-of-fact parts of every day life, lead to sustained harmony and balance. Until appropriate response to conflict is learned throughout the world, literal fences and walls are needed. But everyone has the power to remove the figurative walls and fences in their lives.

A proactive approach to conflict is healthy and wise and encourages a culture conducive to open discussion. Skills and steps to successful conflict resolution are gained and honed daily as a matter of course. Ignored or badly handled conflict builds (de)fences of helplessness, frustration, distrust and failure. Conflict handled well replaces (de)fences with transformation, reconciliation, empowerment and freedom. When people are free they are empowered. When people are empowered they can reconcile. When people are reconciled they can transform. Transformation leads to transcendence. *Are you up to this challenge?*

CHAPTER FIVE

Living the Creative Life
It ain't easy, but it's worth it!

Darla Arni

Over the past 20 years, Darla has energized and motivated thousands of people. She works with people and organizations that want to be more innovative and productive in life and work.

She is the author of *Sharing Creativity at Home* and the *Sharing Creative Energy* newsletter. Darla's work and experiences have been featured on MSNBC's online magazine, in regular segments on the Fox Morning Show in Kansas City, and in her nationwide column and e-newsletter.

As a professional speaker, writer, columnist, television personality, multitasking wife and mom Darla awakens sleeping creativity and brings a renewed sense of power and commitment to everyone she meets.

Darla offers keynote presentations, half- and full- day seminars and "Playing With A Purpose" activities on:

- The Creative Mindset
- Creativity Killers
- Creating Time and Balance
- Custom designed Teambuilding & Corporate Games

Sharing Creative Energy
Slater, MO 65349 • 660-529-2969 • www.darlaarni.com

Darla Arni

Living the Creative Life
It ain't easy, but it's worth it!

Once there was a woman who loved her job, her co-workers, and even loved her salary. But there was a problem—her boss. Her boss made her work environment so miserable that she felt there was only one solution: quit her job. In search of a new job she went to see a headhunter. None of the jobs she heard about seemed to fit, and even though she was unhappy, she still loved her present job.

Just when she thought she couldn't stand one more day, a light bulb went off in her head. Aha! A solution! She went back to the headhunter but this time she gave him her boss's name and resume. In no time at all, the headhunter found her boss a new job. Her boss was happy to take it because he wasn't really happy either. She got to keep the job she loved. In time she was promoted to her old boss's position and lived happily ever after. Was this woman being creative? You bet she was, and it worked!

Everyone has the capacity to be innovative and creative. According to Dr. Teresa Amabile, a psychologist at Brandeis University who researches creativity, "We've become narrow in the ways we think about creativity. We tend to think of creativity as rarefied: artists are creative, musicians are creative, and so are poets and filmmakers. But the chef in her kitchen is also showing creativity when she invents a variation on a recipe."

How do we reach the point of using creativity in our everyday lives? To start, forget about trying to think outside of the proverbial "box" and work on getting outside of yourself. Any boxes we find ourselves in have been built by our own negative self-talk and self-imposed limitations. But no matter where you live, work, or play, you can increase your creativity by recognizing the following seven barriers to creativity and learning to navigate around them.

Fear of Failure

Have you ever been afraid? It is human nature to avoid failure. No one wants to appear stupid or silly in front of others. Instead of taking even a small risk, many of us choose to stay within our comfort zone. In fact, reward structures within the workplace and society are often set up so the punishment for failure is greater than the reward for risking success. As a result, we become immobilized and conditioned to take the safe way out. While we are busy being safe, the possibility for learning and growing is lost, and creativity goes out the window. As Albert Einstein put it, "A person who never made a mistake never tried anything new."

Order and Tradition

Order and tradition go hand in hand and keep us doing things the way they have always been done. While tradition produces stability, it also produces stagnancy. It is no wonder that the following phrases have been heard when someone dares to step out of line and offer up a new way of doing things:

- We tried that before.
- Don't rock the boat.
- It'll never fly.
- You can't teach an old dog new tricks.
- People don't want change.
- We've always done it this way.

How about you? Jot down other phrases you can think of that are used to keep creative people in line.

_____

_____

_____

_____

Personal Nearsightedness

Have you ever searched for something and when you finally found it realized it had been right in front of you the entire time? That's what personal nearsightedness is like. It is a failure to see your own abilities and strengths and the value of people around you. Many of us develop creative tunnel vision and don't appreciate the differences and unique talents and contributions of friends, family members, and co-workers.

For example, it is often difficult for us to see someone we grew up with as an expert in his or her chosen field. How could that be? We've known them all our lives and they are nothing special! This also explains why, no matter what your age, you can still become a little child around your parents. Nearsightedness is most often seen among practical, no-nonsense people who only see things as they really are or as they used to be. In contrast, innovative and creative people thrive on seeing things as they could be or might be. Which are you?

Overcertainty

Can you ever really be 100% sure of something? Sometimes we think so. Even experts in their fields can be reluctant to try new ideas. The old method worked, they were publicly rewarded for it, and they don't want to give it up. This can happen to us, too. We get stuck in the old ways of doing things, resisting new approaches. We live in a fast-paced world, and to presume that what we knew yesterday still applies can be a huge mistake.

That's why innovation and change frequently come from outside our group of friends, family, or work associates. Consider the opinions of these one-time experts:

*The horse is here to stay, but the automobile
is only a novelty—a fad.*

– President of the Michigan Savings Bank advising Henry Ford's
lawyer not to invest in the Ford Motor Company

*Video won't be able to hold on to any market it captures
after the first six months. People will soon get tired of
staring at a plywood box every night.*

– Daryl F. Zanuck, head of 20th Century Fox movie studio
commenting on television in 1946

Look at your own life. Are you clinging to old ideas and outmoded methods?

Lack of Forcefulness

Do you see yourself as a take-charge person or as one who gives in easily to outside opinions? The most innovative people aren't always the most forceful. They might have a great idea but lack the gumption to stand up for their own beliefs. On the other hand, the most forceful people may be stuck in a rut with old ideas but be pushy enough to overrun everyone else. In either case, good ideas are lost along the way. A group is only as creative as its most dominant members. Have you ever seen this happen in an organization? Are you one of those with good, creative ideas that is afraid to speak up? Are you forceful, but stuck?

Lack of Playfulness

A child can play with a paper towel tube for at least an hour. It becomes a telescope, a horn, a tunnel for small cars, a magic wand, a baseball bat and more. We expect children to learn through play, but as adults we're supposed to be serious, right? Wrong! Play is a method of learning and experimenting that works for adults, too. I believe we take ourselves too seriously and plan our entire lives with the end product in mind instead of focusing on the process of our experiences along the way.

Playfulness has its place in every facet of your life. Through play you can try out new skills, explore "what if" questions and bring new energy and exuberance to dull, stagnant environments. I believe in the power of play so much that I often tell my audiences that my next product will be bumper stickers that say, "Goofy is Good." Are you ready to add a little play to your day?

Too Many Rewards

Is it possible to be rewarded too much? Yes, say the experts, if creativity is the goal. When the rewards are great and the stakes are high, people tend to focus on the rewards instead of the intrinsic pleasure of the creative activity. To be creative you must take risks. If you are rewarded, that is great. If not, it doesn't really matter.

Lack of creativity often happens in the television industry, where the payoffs are huge. Creative programming tends to come from educational television or other small settings instead of networks that stick to tried-and-true formulas to bring in the big bucks. Have you ever squelched a creative idea because you wanted to play it safe? How did you feel about it afterward?

Regaining Your Creative Mindset

Now that you know what to avoid, here are three steps that will help you regain the creative mindset you were born with and keep it alive forever. Is it easy? NO! Is it worth it? YES! Let's get started.

Step 1: Mindfulness

Mindfulness is being attentive without thinking, without analyzing, and without feeling. It is learning to live in the moment, in the NOW and focus without distraction. In our day-to-day life it means:

- Don't finish sentences for others.

- Don't be thinking at breakfast what you are going to have for lunch.

- Don't spend all your time making lists of what you are supposed to be doing instead of actually doing something.

And that's just for starters.

Many of us walk around in a daze that consists of mulling over events of the past and mapping out a plan for the future instead of attending to the present, which is the only true place we exist. Consciously paying attention slows us down and makes us more efficient, productive, and energetic. By paying attention to everything in the moment you will become aware of details, intuitions, and innovative solutions that would otherwise have been lost in the shuffle.

Being mindful engages all of your senses. Can you recall your ride to work? Do you notice when a co-worker gets a haircut? Do you find yourself asking people to repeat things even though there is nothing wrong with your hearing? One of the easiest ways to be more mindful is by learning how to listen. Remember that hearing is the capacity to receive the sounds; listening is the act of paying attention to the sounds themselves.

To increase your daily mindfulness, try these listening skills activities:

- Make a concerted effort to keep your mouth closed and listen to someone else talk without interrupting. We all have fantastic opinions and enlightening things to say, but don't express them at the expense of cutting into someone else's time to speak. If you are like me, this can be an embarrassing eye-opener. Being quiet and listening to another person without trying to put in your two cents can be a challenge, especially when you are a professional speaker!

- Sit back, close your eyes, lay your hands in your lap and rely only on your sense of hearing for five minutes. What do you hear? More importantly, of what sounds are you aware that you normally take for granted, and what conclusions can you make from the sounds you hear? Make a list of what you heard and repeat this exercise periodically. You not only will become more aware and attuned to your environment, but you also will be giving yourself a relaxing moment to recharge.

Learning to quietly exist with oneself can be challenging. Our world is set up to keep us constantly entertained and engaged, allowing for little creativity. According to organizational development specialist Don Prentice, "The essence of creativity is to listen. You have to listen. Just forget yourself, whoever that is; leave yourself open and let it be. That's creativity."

Step 2: Ask Dumb Questions

It has been said that there are no dumb questions, but most of us wish someone else would ask them first! I propose that in order for us to learn and grow, life should be a questioning process. Creative people are curious people who are interested in many things. I often wish I had the nine lives of a cat because there are many directions I would like to go with my life and not enough time to explore them all.

An ancient Asian technique of asking why five times leads to some interesting discoveries. For example:

I slept late this morning. Why?

Because I was up till 2 a.m. Why?

Because I had work to finish. Why?

Because I had to meet an important deadline. Why?

Because I didn't want to get in trouble at work. Why?

Because my boss scares me.

By applying this "5 x Why" technique to some of your everyday actions and activities, you might discover there are things you do and keep on doing for no good reason. By eliminating needless activities you free time for more meaningful, productive endeavors. A creative life is a continual quest and good questions are useful guides. Asking dumb questions helps you overcome the traps of order and tradition, personal nearsightedness, and overcertainty. Think how different our lives would be if these questions were never asked.

- Bill Bowerman (inventor of Nike shoes): What happens if I pour rubber into my waffle iron?

- Godfrey Hounsfield (inventor of the CAT scanner): Why can't we see in three dimensions what is inside a human body without cutting it open?

- Masaru Ibuka (honorary chairman, Sony): Why don't we remove the recording function and speaker and put headphones in the recorder? (Result: the Sony Walkman.)

Your challenge:

Each day for a week, take a few minutes to ask yourself a question that begins with "I wonder." Keep an I wonder journal so you can review your list periodically. If you have trouble coming up with your own I wonder list, e-mail me and ask for my "Wonderful List of Wonders" to get you started. (Go to page 63 to get started.)

Step 3: Gain Control of Your Mind Chatter

Right now as you read this page, what are you thinking? You may not realize it, but every waking moment your brain is filled with mind chatter. This internal conversation is framing the way you see yourself and everything that happens to you, and most of it is negative and judgmental. Your mind chatter, or whatever you choose to call it, makes you feel both afraid to do something and guilty if you don't. Much of your negative self-talk is from past messages and judgments drilled into you by people that don't even matter in your life anymore.

Research shows that even a slight decrease in your negative self-talk increases your ability to respond to the world more creatively. To take control of your mind chatter you must first become aware of what it is telling you. You can discover the ratio of negative messages to positive messages by using some of the following techniques.

- Keep a journal or tally of positive thoughts versus negative thoughts. Begin by trying it for just one day, and then expand it to a week. What did you discover? Often the ratio of negative to positive is 4 to 1 or even 8 to 1.

- Use a golf counter to keep track of only the negative messages you give yourself throughout the day. For example, can you look in a mirror without being critical of how you look? While you go about your day are you constantly berating yourself for being too slow, too fast, not good enough, or a bad parent? Try not to look at the total until the end of the day.

- Wear a rubber band around your left wrist if you are right-handed or your right wrist if you are left-handed. Each time you catch yourself thinking negatively, pull on the rubber band and give yourself a flick. I guarantee this will wake you up and make you take notice! If your wrist is red and swollen at the end of the day you know your negatives outweigh your positives.

With this newfound awareness comes creative change. We can control our thoughts instead of letting our thoughts control us. The following are techniques you can use to break the negative self-talk cycle:

- Mentally yell "Stop," and switch your thoughts to another subject. Yell it out loud if necessary or tell the negative voice to "Get out!"

- Get up and exercise. Go for a short walk. Change your scenery and just move! Schedule regular exercise and activity into your week. Rarely do people experience negative mind chatter about themselves or others while they are physically active. As an added bonus, regular exercise has been proven to increase concentration and decrease depression.

- Objectively question the logic of your negative messages with curiosity. Instead of accepting the judgment "I always make wrong decisions" challenge it with "What are some decisions I've made that turned out to be good?" Negative messages mask themselves as reality, but when held up to the facts they can usually be proven wrong.

Gaining control of your negative thoughts helps conquer your fear of failure and lack of forcefulness and frees you to be more playful and fun.

Take Charge

You now know the creative barriers to avoid. You are armed with tools that will enable you to overcome the barriers and bring a new level of creativity and innovation to your life. As I said at the beginning of this chapter, forget about trying to get out of the proverbial "box" and concentrate on getting outside of yourself. You are responsible for your own experiences and choices—no excuses and no blaming.

Nothing can stop you now! As you begin to live a more creative life, friends, family, and co-workers will see the difference. More importantly, you will feel better about yourself, you will feel energized, and you will be able to overcome temporary setbacks because you see the creative way out.

Creativity can solve almost any problem. The creative act, the defeat of habit by originality, overcomes everything.

– George Lois (legendary advertising executive and artist)

References for a creative life:

Take the Road to Creativity and Get Off your Dead End, by David Campbell (Argus Communications 1977)

The Creative Spirit, by Daniel Goleman, Paul Kaufman, and Michael Ray (Dutton 1992)

I Wonder ...

CHAPTER SIX

Rx for Friendship
Just what the doctor ordered

Paula Baum
and
Susan Concannon

Paula Baum and Susan Concannon share a passion for their friendship. Although they met only 10 years ago, their relationship quickly progressed from acquaintance to good friends to their present status as "best friends." What makes their situation unique is the fact that they live three hours apart. With the encouragement of their families and friends they recently embarked on a new relationship as business partners in the world of professional speaking, and thus Two of a Kind was born.

Married to physicians for over 20 years and each the mother of three children, these fun, energetic and motivational women share their personal stories along with their suggestions for improving and deepening your relationships in a style that entertains and delights audiences. With Paula's nursing background and Susan's degree in psychology, they blend information from adolescence to the golden years in their presentation *Rx for Friendship*.

Two of a Kind
PO Box 189, Beloit, KS 67420 • 785-841-1246 • www.weare2ofakind.com

Paula Baum and Susan Concannon

Rx for Friendship

Just what the doctor ordered

What do you call a cheerleader, Dear Abby, a fashion consultant, a business partner, a lunch date, a shoulder to cry on, a diary full of your deepest secrets and all your favorite stuff rolled into one? Your girlfriend, or course!

People form friendships in different walks of life. These are the people you know from church, school activities, work, the fitness center, and so on. Although these relationships might be important to you, unless you get together outside of the original setting and share experiences with one another, the friendship will not progress.

There are women who, for one reason or another, are not comfortable with intimacy. They are satisfied with "acquaintance" relationships because they are safe. Emotionally they risk very little, but by the same token, they will never know what they are missing.

Those that do progress, move on to yet another level of intimacy, becoming close friends. The desire for trust, love and intimacy is at the heart of all close relationships. A person might have several close friends in her lifetime. These are the friends you enjoy being with and can depend on in times of need. These friends are loyal. It has been said that friends are the family you choose for yourself.

Occasionally a best friend rises above the rest. It could be a lifelong acquaintance or someone you met recently. She is more than a companion. This is the friend you trust with your innermost secrets. It is being known and accepted and understood to the core. A best friend is someone who gives without keeping lists and who receives gifts with gratitude. It is as though there is a spiritual connection. Jan Yager, Ph.D., states that a best friend "provides a window into the soul of another." Finding such a friend is not always easy, but when you do you have indeed been blessed.

We are careful not to overuse the term "soul mate". It should be reserved for that truly special connection. For those of us who are married, we cannot discuss a soul mate without thinking of our husbands. What a wonderful way to feel about your spouse! With that said, we encourage you to seek female friendships outside your marriage. In the book *Friendship Factor*, Alan L. McGinnis states: "Your marriage ought to be the finest friendship you have, but not the only one." We cannot expect one person to fulfill all of our friendship needs. For those lucky enough to be in a happy, healthy relationship, having at least one best friend who is the consummate soul mate is what most people ultimately strive for.

Our Prescription

Everyone has the potential to find a soul mate, or kindred spirit. The trick is maintaining that friendship. Our prescription for friendship will empower you to make new friends and deepen current friendships. Our prescription is:

> **F**un Factor
> **R**evealing Oneself
> **I**nescapable Gender Differences
> **E**ncourage Each Other
> **N**ourish With Warmth
> **D**emonstrate Acts of Kindness
> **S**pace – It's A Good Thing
> **H**ighlight Her Assets
> **I**mprove Communication by Listening
> **P**rioritize

Fun Factor

This is what brings us together and keeps us sane! Studies show that one of the most sought after qualities in a friend is the ability to have fun together. Of course it is! We all love to laugh and we love the people who make us laugh.

Health professionals have known for some time that humor helps reduce anxiety, opens up communication, gives support and serves as a safety valve for both frustration and anger. As in the movie *Patch Adams,* physicians and hospitals have made an effort to integrate humor into the wellness plan for their patients. Laughter truly is the best medicine.

We are now finding that not just laughter, but the friendship package as a whole, helps the body's autoimmune system resist disease. Friends help us live better. Friends help us eat and sleep better. Those of us with close friendships are more apt to take prescribed medications, make and keep checkups with our doctors and generally take better care of our health. Like the saying goes, "There is no physician like a true friend."

Health benefits aside, it is important to just have fun. A friendship that is all talk, always intense, all about sharing your deepest thoughts and consistently focused on problems, feels like a therapy session with your shrink. Although those conversations are important, you need to mix it up a little. Sharing fun experiences creates memories. You never know what tomorrow will bring and what special memories will sustain you through difficult times.

The Swedes have a saying:

Shared joy is double joy,
and shared sorrow is half sorrow.

Rx: St. Jane's Wort – An essential extract that promotes a positive mood and maintains a healthy and happy outlook on life. Take as needed for kicks and giggles.

Revealing Oneself

Honesty can literally be a health insurance policy. Confiding in a close friend helps reduce the stresses of everyday life and we are much less likely to become depressed. Research shows that people who have friends cut their risk of death by more than 60 percent. Also, a UCLA study shows that *not* having a good friend is as big a health risk as obesity or smoking.

Honesty is a steppingstone to move from acquaintance to friend. If you take that first step and reveal a part of yourself, she will be more likely to share a secret. The key to honesty and revealing oneself is trust. You *must* honor her confidence with complete privacy.

Another advantage of revealing oneself is the opportunity to improve your own self-esteem. If you are able to share a part of your "darker side" and discover that she accepts you and still likes you, you will be more capable of forgiving yourself. You can put it all behind you and get over it!

Rx: Communication Peel – Apply generously to peel away layers of defensiveness, negativity and insecurities. When used as directed will lead to self-disclosure and a healthier, more intimate relationship.

Inescapable Gender Differences

Men and women, as in most things, differ in how they perceive friendship. Men's friendships are based on activities and shared interests. Women base friendships on feelings and shared values. These differences give women the opportunity to have more intimate relationships that fulfill their emotional and intellectual needs. Considering this, it is amazing that in ancient Greece women were considered too ignorant and uneducated to be capable of a meaningful friendship. We've come a long way, baby!

So while our husbands are out fishing or playing golf, we are spending quality time with a friend, sharing our innermost thoughts and secrets. This leads to self-knowledge and an inner peace that many men never realize.

Rx: Friendamycin – Provides the awareness and acceptance that men and women approach relationships differently. Take the full amount prescribed to achieve a healthy balance between the sexes.

Encourage Each Other

The Army says "Be all that you can be!" but we say, "You go, girl!" Be your friend's biggest cheerleader! We suggest:

1. Emphasize her uniqueness. Urge her to be herself. People have a way of becoming what you encourage them to be, not what you nag them to be.

2. Criticize with care. Never delight in sharing your critical thoughts. Remember that truth without love is brutal and cruel.

3. Honor her personality, quirks and all. Understanding there will be things that irritate you is a first step in accepting and enjoying who she is.

4. Allow her the freedom to make her own choices. You may not agree with her choice; nevertheless, be supportive.

Rx: Cheeragra – Take as needed to be a positive influence and to inspire your friend to bigger and better things. Produces a nurturing environment for her to grow.

Nourish with Warmth

Have you ever had a massage? If you have, remember that glowing sensation that lasted for hours afterwards? If you haven't, call and make an appointment today!

People are born with a desire to be touched and held. Pressure from society gradually stops the hand holding, hugging and other innocent forms of displaying affection. We do not believe that the American way is the right way in this instance. In fact, research shows that skin is our most powerful sense organ. There are times of grief and times of happiness when words cannot convey the profound emotion being felt. It takes a hug! We encourage you to defy the social stigma of touching. Use your body to express warmth.

It is important when hugging to not overdo it. A hug-o-maniac often offends people and invades their personal space. If the situation calls for a handshake rather than a hug, go with that instead. Whatever you do, keep it genuine.

Rx: Pal-o'-mine Lotion – Apply liberally to skin to express interest and affection. Guaranteed to produce a warm, healthy glow.

Demonstrate Acts of Kindness

"Ask not what your friend can do for you, but what you can do for your friend." Okay…we know that's not exactly what JFK said, but we give him special credit for inspiring us. When you have a close or best friend, you are inspired to do nice things for them.

One of the best ways to deepen friendships is by doing for others. Of course you will remember your friend's birthday and honor her family's special days; however, friendship needs no special occasion.

Express kindness with a:

Phone call
Handwritten note
Lunch date
Thoughtful gift

Gifts need not be extravagant or expensive. They do need to represent your desire to bring a moment of happiness to her life. She will value the gift, but more importantly, treasure what it represents. As author Colleen Sell said, "The real gift is the friendship."

Rx: Worth Control Pills – Take daily. Do not skip a single day or opportunity to demonstrate love and appreciation for your friend.

Space ...It's a Good Thing!

Have you ever had a friend that wanted to be included in everything you do? She wanted your friendship to be exclusive? How did that make you feel?

There is such a thing as too much closeness. How can fond memories be relished if you are never apart? The mark of a mature relationship is allowing your friend room to breathe. Don't suffocate one another. It is healthy to have other friendships, so don't be threatened by them. Jealousy is negative and crippling to your relationship. Don't get caught in the trap of the "Green Eyed Monster."

Rx: Envystat – Take daily. Repeat as needed until fulfilled, content and no longer thirsting for exclusive rights to your friend. To be used to help control jealousy and other symptoms of monopolizing friend disease.

Highlight Her Assets

I can live two full months on one good compliment.

– Mark Twain

Praise your friend and watch her flourish. We have known this about raising children for years, but everyone needs positive strokes. You may hold someone in high regard, but unless you tell her, how will she ever know? A friend is not a mind reader. It is important that you express words of affirmation. Your friend will love you all the more for your good taste!

Extend your praise beyond your best friend, spouse, close friends and acquaintances. Share a kind word with a drive-up window clerk and watch his or her body language improve. An unexpected compliment is frequently the most valued. We hear so many negative things in our society, that a word of praise will long be remembered. Each of us can surely recall a compliment on a haircut, new shoes, neat handwriting, and so on. It gives an energetic boost and makes your outlook more positive. A person who feels good about herself and likes herself is friendlier to be around. So go ahead, make her day!

Rx: Niceyderm Patch – Apply daily to clean, dry skin. Used to train people to express appreciation for their friends' positive attributes. The end result provides a source of affirmation that increases self-esteem in those you care most about.

Improve Communication By Listening

A good listener is always popular and more intimate with friends. When it comes to listening, most of us agree that this is an area in which we can improve.

Some hints for being a good listener are:

- Concentrate on what is being said. It is important that you are listening and not thinking about what you will say next.

- Listen with your eyes! Look at a person when they are speaking. Your eyes give away your interest level. If you are looking around, checking out other people in the room, you are telling the person that what they are saying is not very interesting. Be attentive.

- Give advice sparingly. Even if people ask for it, they often do not want the advice. The person just appreciates you for listening. This gives them an opportunity to sort things out and see a situation more clearly for themselves.

- Confidentiality! As mentioned before, *never* break a confidence.

- Respond appropriately. It might be a question, a comment, or just a laugh, but an appropriate response shows that you are listening and that you value what is being said.

Rx: Nitrolistener – Tablet should be placed under the tongue to assist in "holding" it when necessary.

Prioritize

Do your friendships rank as one of the most important assets in your life? Most women answer, "Absolutely." Those same women, however, try to fit their friends in between family, work, church, housework, groceries, fitness activities, clubs... well, you get the drift. Your friendships deserve a better time slot. It is such an honor to have a friend. Give it the attention necessary to not just maintain, but to deepen the friendship. As Jan Yager advises, avoid letting a cherished friendship fade simply because of poor time management or neglect. It takes effort. You might have to schedule times to get together for lunch, take a walk or even squeeze in a phone call. By keeping the lines of communication open, you keep the friendship growing. Just do what you have to do and don't put your friend on the back burner of life.

Some suggestions:

- Set a time for lunch once a month. If it doesn't work out, be sure to reschedule.
- When you speak on the phone, suggest another time to talk or get together.
- Take walks together.
- Go with each other to appointments. The waiting room is a lot less miserable if you can visit with a friend.

Rx: Timeatap – Take as needed to locate that extra time in your busy week to spend with your friend.

This concludes our Prescription for Friendship. Treat this as you would a prescription of penicillin. Take the entire amount. Rather than ten days, continue this prescription for a lifetime. There are no adverse side effects!

There are people in this world that will never need our prescription. You know them. They are the people to whom everyone else is drawn. They are popular and have many friends. What is their secret? These lucky people are naturals at warmth and communication. Like professional athletes, they practice. We amateurs can become that beloved friend. We first have to make the choice, then practice our communication skills and finally take the time necessary for friendship. Remember, friendship is voluntary. It is up to you to treat yourself to this priceless commodity we call friendship.

CHAPTER SEVEN

Diva Days
Say Yes to You!™

Allison Adams Blankenship

Real Life...Real Solutions...Real Fun! is the message in every keynote and seminar with Allison Blankenship. She has been described as a speaker who can reach both heads and hearts.

Combining practical, easy-to-use, hands-on tools with boundless energy, Allison delivers content-rich programs that are fun and entertaining. Her experience includes a 20-year, award-winning career in corporate communications with clients in finance, banking, retail, hospitality, tourism, insurance and healthcare.

In 1996 she founded Life's Simple Solutions, Inc., a motivational training company in Naples, Florida. Allison speaks across the country 150 times a year on strengthening communications, overcoming conflict and reducing stress.

Allison's audiences applaud her humor, sensible strategies and easy-to-apply ideas. She weaves real-life examples of being a successful business professional, consultant, speaker and step-mom of two teenagers throughout her presentations, while giving participants the tools and techniques they need to succeed.

Life's Simple Solutions
Naples, FL • 800-664-7641 • www.AllisonSpeaks.com

Allison Adams Blankenship

Diva Days

Say Yes to You!™

> *Sometimes I get so worn out*
> *being useful that I'm useless.*
>
> – Jan Karon

Does that quote sound familiar? Ever find yourself dreaming of 15 minutes alone with no interruptions? Do you fall asleep during routine tasks like driving or cooking dinner? If so, this chapter is for you!

Traveling throughout the country speaking at women's leadership seminars, I found a disturbing kinship with my fellow sisters—we were all running on emotional empty. We were so busy being everything to everyone else that we lost sight of nurturing ourselves.

It reminded me of a demonstration where a plastic cup is filled with water to represent your life. This "cup of life" is then poured into other cups symbolizing work, family, and friends. We give ourselves to those causes because it makes us feel needed, valued and loved. If we neglect to refill our own cup, it becomes empty and the cup is then shattered into pieces. The same is true for us—when we neglect to refill our own cup by nurturing ourselves, we burn out and eventually break down, too.

How full is your cup of life? Feeling a little empty? The problem of putting other people's needs before yours is that when your cup runs dry, you have nothing left to give to the causes and people you love. It appears to be a Catch-22.

Say Yes to You!™

Women have been socialized into believing that taking care of oneself is selfish—on the contrary! Nurturing yourself and your soul is survival. It is the instinct to love and live, and today you are giving yourself permission to take care of you. It is impossible to have a fulfilled life without "Saying Yes to You!"

Oh, I couldn't, you exclaim. What will people think?! Let's consider what happens when you do not address your needs:

- Heart disease is the number one killer of women. It is even ahead of cancer. More women die from heart attacks than men because women dismiss or ignore the symptoms—they are too busy taking care of everyone else.

- The average business loses one to four days of productivity per employee per year because the employees are too stressed to be fully functional.

- The *Wall Street Journal* reports that the lack of personal and professional balance is one of the top six reasons new managers fail.

- A Yale University study found a direct correlation between the body's reaction to stress and the amount of fat in the stomach area. Stress stimulates cortisol production, which in turn, pumps fat into the stomach area, increasing the risk of heart disease and strokes—not to mention the fact that you can't zip up your pants!

- And the *American Journal of Pharmacology* reported that in 1999, 85% of all prescriptions written were for anti-depressants. We are becoming a society of stress addicts and it is literally killing us.

Look at Say Yes to You™ with a Diva Day this way: taking care of you guarantees that you will be there for the others you love and take care of.

Determining Your Diva Delights

Ready to indulge in a little diva "divine-ness"? The best guarantee to get the time you need to replenish your soul is to create a ritual that you can schedule in advance. By establishing a daily, weekly or monthly ritual, your family and friends eventually understand that you are unavailable during that time. The first few tries may be awkward, but by the third time you indulge in your ritual, they will get the message!

Here are some fun ideas to get you started on your own diva-deemed ritual schedule:

- Treat tired feet with a soothing soak at the end of the week. Take a large shallow plastic tub and cover the bottom with glass marbles. Fill the tub with warm water and add your favorite bubble bath or aromatherapy oil. Gently roll your feet along the marbles for a relaxing foot massage.

- Start a family tradition with a weekend nap or morning sleep-in. If the family objects, offer a treat—rent a favorite video for the kids to watch quietly while you nap, or cook a special breakfast after your sleep-in and invite friends for your kids with the understanding it's a special sleep-in event.

- Escape reality with a fun novel or magazine at lunch. Squirrel yourself away for 20 minutes with a favorite read that you've wanted to explore. Pick up that grocery-store tabloid or trashy novel—just be careful who sees you reading it at work!

- Enjoy a holistic cleansing soak. Pour one cup each of Epsom salts and baking soda into warm bath water. Feel free to add a few drops of lavender or peppermint oil and then relax for 20 minutes. You'll feel refreshed and cleansed by the salts extracting impurities out through your skin.

- Create a little quality time with your family with a picnic at home. Be creative by laying a tablecloth on the floor or popping a tent indoors. Have easy-to-eat finger foods or introduce a new treat especially for this event. Schedule it in advance so that your children can look forward to it.

- Take a night off from cooking without spending a great deal of money. Plan a "leftover lotto" once a week to clean out the refrigerator in a fun way. Arrange all the leftovers by the basic food groups on a counter or table. Then make a slip of paper for each of your family members and number them individually. Throw them in a bowl and draw numbers. Whoever draws number one gets to go through the "buffet line" first! This is one night they can have as much or as little as they want—remember, the goal is to clean out the refrigerator. Number two goes next, followed by number three, etc.

- Set aside a movie day, either at home or at a theatre. Hold an informal movie review afterwards with your friends or family. If at home, have movie treats ready—popcorn, candy, soda—and then snuggle up with a cozy blanket. TNT hosts "Cinematherapy," movies especially for women. Check to see if your cable company carries TNT and schedule a movie night with your best friend.

- Have a girls-night-only event. Take turns at home cooking dinner or hosting a wine or martini tasting event, meet for lunch, have your nails done at the same time, play cards and board games, or start a book club. The important thing is that you schedule some adult female time you can count on and look forward to.

- Swap mini-massages with friends. Take turns soothing the body's most stressed areas: your neck, shoulders and feet. You can use massage or aromatherapy oils to lessen the friction and increase circulation. Add a beauty boost to your feet with cotton socks after your massage. Cotton locks in the moisture of the oil and comforts tired muscles.

Don't be surprised to experience a little resistance by family members and friends to your diva-ness initially. When I first introduced Diva Days to my family, they weren't fully cooperative—until they figured out that when I take personal time, they can, too. This is not a one-sided activity as the family also benefits from a renewed you. Remember the water in the cup demonstration: if you don't take time for you, you won't have the time and energy to give to others.

Sometimes your Diva Day is impromptu—once you get in the habit of investing and nurturing yourself, you become very good at responding to emergency diva situations. At our house, we have a symbol to communicate the need for personal space: a tiara. If I feel the need to treat myself, I don a tiara and sit at my desk. The Fed Ex man thinks I'm nuts when I answer the door, but it makes me laugh and feel a little better. Sometimes

I wear my best rhinestone tiara while doing chores around the house, just to remind me of the true diva within. We even created T-shirts that proclaim "Queen of the Universe", lest anyone forget our diva-ness.

Becoming a Daily Diva

The ultimate goal of Diva Days is to incorporate a little diva into every day. Do you know that 20 minutes a day of diva indulgence over the course of a year equals a college semester's worth of time? Imagine a personal development course designed especially for you that lasts ten weeks! Can't go 20 minutes? Try five. Five minutes a day over the course of a year is almost four full business days. When is the last time you spent that kind of time investing and nurturing yourself? Imagine how your family, friends and loved ones will benefit from the refreshed new you.

Hear are some quick ideas for diva delights five minutes at a time:

- Pop a chocolate. Dark chocolate contains the same feel-good chemicals found in mood stimulants. A study at the University of Bath in England found that people who ate chocolate every day reported being happier than those who did not. And dark chocolate helps lower blood pressure!

- Read the morning paper outside. We are more sensitive to the sun's benefits in the morning. Some researchers believe the sun can help balance hormones to energize you during the day and relax you at night.

- Walk or exercise at lunch or in the morning. Take the stairs instead of the elevator, park your car a little further away and walk to the office or the mall, or practice simple stretching exercises at your desk or in between commercials. Your goal is only five minutes and you'll be pleasantly surprised at how much better you feel.

- Say a bedtime prayer. Dr. David Niven, author of *The 100 Simple Secrets of Happy People* conducted a survey and found that people who pray on a regular basis are much happier than those who do not.

- On that same note, try keeping a blessing journal. Every time you feel tired or depressed, jot down a few of the things for which you are grateful or feel blessed. Oprah calls this her "Attitude of Gratitude" journal.

- Try a "stress shake" to ward off the siesta syndrome. Stand up and extend your arms in front of you, gently shaking your wrists; let the motion travel up your arms to your shoulders. Continue shaking your body down through your hips and very carefully shake out one foot and leg at a time. (You probably want to do this in private! If not, it is guaranteed to get rid of unwanted company.) When you stop, you'll feel a tingling sensation along with a renewed sense of energy. Stress shakes literally shake up your circulation to bring you more oxygen and a great energy boost.

- Pop a vitamin C tablet to fight stress. Researchers at the University of Alabama in Huntsville found that 500-1000 mg daily slashes the production of stress hormones. That equals two eight-ounce glasses of orange juice or a quality supplement.

- Breathe from your abdomen. Proper breathing from your abdomen is a great way to relax tired shoulders and neck tension. Put both feet flat on the floor with one hand on your stomach. Slowly inhale through your nose, filling up your stomach first, followed by your lungs. Then exhale the air through your mouth, releasing carbon dioxide. This is the same carbon dioxide that fills your fat cells to create cellulite, so feel free to do this all throughout the day!

- Snack on an apple. In addition to being loaded with fiber, the scent of apples stimulates an area of the brain associated with happiness and satisfaction. The health benefits are excellent, too: the apple fiber can help with depression and even suppress out-of-control food cravings.

- Put a green dot on your phone—that is your secret reminder to take one deep breath before you answer the phone. Not only will you feel better, you'll sound more confident, too.

Creating a Diva Destiny

Still not convinced that you can *Say Yes to You*™ and take time to refill that cup of life? Consider the message you give your children when they see you take time to replenish your spirit, take care of your health, and balance stress with playfulness—and then consider the message you send when you do not. Jess O'Neil said it best: *"High achievers excel at making a living but often fail at making a life."* Is that how you want to be remembered by your loved ones? By teaching your children that a balanced life includes taking care of yourself, you are giving them the skills to live a fulfilled and productive life.

Becoming a true diva takes daily intention and practice. It also involves a little planning and a lot of attention to your dreams. Start by identifying what is stressing you right now. On a piece of paper, separate your stressors into two columns: on the left, write down those stressors that are inescapable; on the right, the ones over which you have more control. Focus on the right side by prioritizing your immediate needs and remind yourself to let go of items on the left.

Next, write down your personal goals and dreams—include some of those childhood desires and maybe a few silly requests. Your focus here is to reawaken your deepest desires and begin planting seeds of hope to help them grow. Choose one specific goal to work on for the next 12 months and share it with your family or friends. Encourage them to do the same and get together for progress reports every month until the goal is met. You will be surprised at how much energy you have when you take positive steps toward your dreams.

Finally, when guilt attacks, remind yourself that total balance in all areas of your life is a myth. Although others lead us to believe that having it all can be done all at once, the truth is, it cannot. Calvin Coolidge said, *"We cannot do everything at once, but we can do something at once."* Take control over your life by singling out what is most important to you at this stage in your life—family, community, career or friends. Focus on that one aspect and give yourself permission to explore these other areas during the rest of your life.

Then, slap a tiara on your head. At the very least, you'll feel better; at the worst, your family will think you have lost your mind and then, perhaps, they'll leave you alone.

Personal Goals and Dreams

_____

_____

_____

_____

_____

_____

_____

_____

_____

_____

_____

_____

_____

_____

_____

_____

_____

_____

_____

_____

_____

_____

_____

CHAPTER EIGHT

Women Need S.T.R.E.S.S.
(Secrets To Really Effective Sanity Strategies)

Toni Boyles

Toni Boyles, owner of A Place in Time, has over 20 years of experience in the areas of Public Speaking, Human Resource Training and Consulting. She is well known for her personal approach and distinctive methods which include humor, interactive exercises, skills practice and transfer of training strategies. Her style is participant-centered and facilitator led. She believes: "People can change." and that "Training that brings about no change is as effective as a parachute that opens on the first bounce."

She is a graduate of Washburn University with a B.A. in Communications. Before starting her own training company in 1996, Toni worked as a Staff Development Specialist for the Kansas Department of Transportation. She is an active member of the Sales and Marketing Executives of Topeka, ABWA-Kansas Executive Express Network, the Greater Topeka Chamber of Commerce and United Methodist Women.

Toni has many roles in her life: national speaker, trainer, business owner, mother, grandmother, world traveler, volunteer, friend, sister, creative thinker, wife, and humorist. If you were to use one word to describe her in all these roles, it would be simple—*Encourager.*

A Place in Time
Tecumseh, KS • 785-379-8463 • www.tonisplace.com

Toni Boyles

Women Need S.T.R.E.S.S.

(Secrets To Really Effective Sanity Strategies)

Americans represent less than five percent of the world population, yet they buy almost one-third of anti-anxiety pills sold worldwide ($2.3 billion). How many times have you heard or said expressions like *I'm so stressed out, I'm under too much stress or I can't handle all this stress?* I believe stress is epidemic in the Western world. How stressed can you get and still function? Humorist C.W. Metcalf says, "Stress has become our Red Badge of Courage." I agree with him and yet also believe it is necessary to have stress in order to thrive. Finding balance is the challenge.

Stress Truisms

Over the years I have learned some great truths about stress. I believe these truths hold the keys to success in dealing with stressful issues. They help build a healthy baseline and allow us to use sanity strategies successfully. Let's take a look at a couple of them.

What stresses one person brings great joy to another.

My husband David loves almost any kind of car race. It is one of his greatest joys in life. I on the other hand find nothing to love about them. They cause me stress. They are expensive, noisy, dangerous and dirty. David agrees with me on the description yet he still loves them. Not only does he love them, but many others agree with him. Racing is a popular sport all over the world. Enough said? What stresses one person brings great joy to another. This truism demonstrates that you often choose what stresses you. It is important to realize this because if you choose it, you can change it.

It is not the person, event, place or thing that causes us stress. It is our response to the person, event, place or thing.

Part of my time is spent volunteering to teach relationship classes at the Kansas State Women's Correctional Facility. I have learned amazing lessons from those ladies in the last couple of years. Only those with good behavior can attend my classes, but they are a group of very interesting women.

Recently I was at the copy machine making certificates and one of the ladies was assisting me. It offered us some one-on-one time that I rarely got with them. We briefly discussed her situation. She talked of the blessing prison had been for her. She spoke of it as the opportunity she had never had in the outside world. She felt as though she had learned a lot about herself and had time to study the Bible and pray. It had changed her life in a positive way. It was her perception that being in prison was a great blessing. I was blown away. She had offered me such a powerful real-life example of this truism.

What Are Your Stressors?

Take time to identify your personal stressors. Consider those that are internal and external. If you are to practice new strategies, it is necessary to recognize when you need to apply them. Notice I have limited the number of lines. I do not want this chapter to cause you stress, so don't list all of them.

_____   _____

_____   _____

_____   _____

_____   _____

_____   _____

How do you know you are stressed?

Make a list of the things that happen to signal "I'm feeling stressed." Put them in the different realms such as physical (headache), mental (confusion), emotional (anger) and behavioral (yelling). Recognizing stressors when they happen alerts you and creates an awareness of the choices you are making.

Physical	Mental	Emotional	Behavioral
_____	_____	_____	_____
_____	_____	_____	_____
_____	_____	_____	_____

Sanity Strategies

One definition of insanity is repeating the same behavior over and over and expecting a different outcome. With that in mind, ask yourself these questions. Are you really interested in sanity strategies? Do you want to deal more productively with stress? Have you made up your mind that you are in charge of your choices and behaviors? Are you ready to use different behaviors? If so, read on. You will not only find things to ponder, but ideas to put into practice right away.

There are no magic answers here. This is not a complete list of strategies and none are better than others. Each one is needed at different times in different situations by different people. Notice that some are short-term and others are lifelong. We need both to survive the stressors we face in today's world. Decide which ones work for you and when.

Breathe – Relaxation exercises involve slowing down your breathing. It may seem too simple to be effective, but what can you lose by trying it? A few nice deep breaths can be relaxing and a quick and easy stress reliever. You can do this anytime, anywhere. It is not visible to others. It costs nothing. Try it. Post a sign saying "Breath Slow" in the area where you spend most of your time.

New technologies are also available to help reduce stress. Recently I read about RESPeRATE. It is an FDA-cleared, non-drug, medical device proven to lower high blood pressure with no side effects. It is technology that reportedly helps you learn to breathe better. I am not endorsing it as I have never seen or used it. Who would have guessed, though, there was technology to help us reduce stress through slower breathing? I believe most of us can learn to do it ourselves with a little practice.

Reframe Situations – At the age of 19 I got my first speeding ticket. A Kansas Highway Patrolman pulled me over. I was devastated. I was not a rule breaker and thoughts of jail time passed through my mind. I hate to admit it, but I cried. Maybe it would be better described as sobbing hysterically. The poor man did his best to calm me. Not an easy task. He refused to let me drive away until I had myself together. He repeated over and over again "A ticket is so much better than a wreck." At the time his wise counsel fell on deaf ears.

Years have passed and now this technique is one of my favorites to use. It is called reframing. Step back and look at an issue in relationship to the big picture. Will it matter in a week or month? Is it a real problem or just an inconvenience? How could it be worse? Putting a different frame on things often keeps them from even getting on my stress radar screen. Go back to the list of stressors you made and decide if they are really problems or just inconveniences. See if you can reframe some of them right now.

Use Humor – A learned skill that I developed late in life is my sense of humor. The ability to access humor in adversity has single-handedly kept me sane on more than one occasion. A wonderful teacher for me in the use of humor was a lady named Claudia Washington. I met Claudia when I was doing AIDS educational programs for the local school district. She was HIV positive and had been for years when I met her. To say she had a sense of humor and spunk would be an understatement. She modeled a great sense of humor throughout her life and even in her death. She knew she was dying and planned her own service. It was a mixture of funny and sad stories that produced laughter and tears. What a great gift she gave to all of us—the courage and permission to laugh when we wanted to cry. Laughter is a great stress reliever. Learn not to take things so seriously. Practice not taking yourself so seriously. There are a tremendous number of resources in this area. Search the Internet for the words "humor" and "health" for a start. Also, if you do not have a humor buddy, get one. I have a number of them. They are essential for good mental and physical health.

Give Yourself a Timeout – Can you imagine watching a football or soccer game where no one gets a timeout? I doubt if the players would be very effective or the games would last very long. Do you go for hours on end without a timeout? Makes very little sense doesn't it? Timeouts need to be planned. Start scheduling them for yourself right away. Life is not a race. Slow down.

Simplify Your Life – In today's fast-paced 24/7 world it is easy to become overwhelmed. Make a list of the things you could do to simplify each area of your life. What things can you reduce or eliminate? When it comes to making decisions ask yourself, "Will it simplify or complicate my life?" If the answer is complicate, then make sure the benefits outweigh the price you will pay (and I do not mean monetarily). Overwhelmed can mean overstressed. One of my favorite quotes is by Oprah Winfrey:

> *Before you agree to do anything that might add even
> the smallest amount of stress to your life, ask yourself:
> What is my truest intention? Give yourself time to let a
> yes resound within you. When it's right, I guarantee
> that your entire body will feel it.*

I agree.

Behave Like an Iris – In Kansas you can drive down the back roads and find old farm houses and barns that are dilapidated and falling down. If you look closely you may also find a batch of iris growing there. It is amazing how strong they are. A former neighbor of mine hated them so much he dug a deep hole and buried the patch he had. It took a couple of years, but they came back up thicker and stronger than before. Go ahead. Think of yourself as an iris. You can choose to behave like an iris. The next time you are down for the count, just think of the iris and push yourself back up.

Examine Your Values, Commitments and Priorities in Life – Because priorities can change almost daily, this is an activity you need to do several times a year. If what you value and where you spend your time and energy are not congruent, you are going to be overstressed. If you say your family is your most important priority, yet most of your time goes into your social life or career, you will have stress. Priorities and time will never be perfectly aligned. It is an issue we all need to be self aware of on an ongoing basis. Mahatma Gandhi said it best: "Happiness is when what you think, what you say, and what you do are in harmony."

Eliminate Toxic Thoughts from Your Mind – Stress is caused by the things we allow into our minds. Making good choices in this area will go a long way toward achieving good mental health. Toxic thoughts come from many different places—what we read, music, movies, television and people we interact with—just to mention a few. Not only should we avoid negative toxic things, but we should seek out uplifting and inspiring things to plant in our minds. Learn to identify toxic things and run the other direction. Your mental and physical health depend on it.

Eliminate Toxic People and Relationships from Your Life – This one is not as simple as removing toxic stuff or garbage. Working on relationships with people is a lifetime activity and I do not believe in giving up easily. However, there comes a time when we must protect ourselves or our loved ones from toxic people and relationships. This is not a strategy to take lightly. You may be thinking about a spouse, child, parent, friend, sibling or co-worker. Do not make quick or angry decisions here. It is one that requires thought, prayer and wise counsel.

Consider Lifestyle Changes – In other words, take better care of yourself. This is not new information. You have heard it before, but sometimes we need to hear something several times before it sinks in. Stop smoking. Limit the use of alcohol, caffeine, sugar, and high-fat foods. Be honest about the amount of exercise and sleep you get. Are they the right amounts for you? Choose healthy foods for meals and avoid overeating. See your doctor on a regular basis and listen to his or her guidance. Work less, develop hobbies and just take care of yourself. In case you haven't noticed, no one else is going to do this for you.

Examine Irrational Beliefs – Do you have any irrational beliefs? My guess is that you do. I hear several on a regular basis from participants in my classes. Here are a few common ones: *making mistakes is terrible; strong people do not ask for help; I can't change the way I think; things* *ought to be fair; other people make me do things; things should last for-ever*. These beliefs are not only irrational they are self-defeating. Write down your irrational beliefs. Initiate a conversation with a wise person you trust and discuss this list with them.

Make a Joy List – Too many times we focus on what is not going well. Sit down right now and make a joy list. What brings great joy and happiness to your life? Write it down. Read it often. This is also called a gratitude journal. It is an awesome experience to do this at the end of every day. Look for more things to add to your list. Believe it or not, you find what you look for. Try this simple exercise. Look around where you are now and see if you can find something yellow or red. If there are people around, look for glasses or jewelry. Go ahead and do it. No one will know. Did you find any of the things I suggested? My guess is you did. Were they there before? Yes. You just did not notice them because you were not looking for them. It works that way with joy and despair. Be careful what you look for.

Find Support – We all need people to support us. Keep this in mind as you choose your support people. They should not be people who will whine and snivel with you. That is not support. You know whom whiners and snivelers hang out with, don't you? Yes, it is other whiners and snivelers. If you find yourself in the middle of several of them, it should be a wake up call. A real support person expects emotionally mature behavior from you and will let you know when your behavior is in question. Find several of those people.

This seems like the perfect time to mention the issue of seeking pro-fessional help. There are times when the very best strategy for being overstressed is to seek professional counsel. I am aware there is a stigma to doing this. I can't change that. I encourage you to consider this as an option. It might be your physician, minister, or some other trusted profes-sional. Most of us seek counsel in difficult times but we usually consult with friends or family. There is nothing wrong with friends and family, but they are not a substitute for a trained and neutral counselor. It is a myth that strong people do not ask for help. Give yourself permission to do this when necessary.

Final Thoughts

One last thing to consider in this quest for balanced stress is your attitude. It is fundamental to long-term stress management. The frontal lobe has a tendency to organize itself around our goal-directed intentions. If you expect a stressful, tense future then you will probably get it. If you see your future as bright, hopeful, and healthy, then the frontal lobe will seek out the inputs that build your future along the lines of your expectations. In other words, you find what you look for. Look for joy and balance in your life. Go for the S.T.R.E.S.S.!

CHAPTER NINE

Oh Behave!
Etiquette essentials for women on the go

Ann E. Mah, M.S.

Ann Mah, owner of Discover! Strategies and Compass Series Publishing, works with women's organizations across the nation on strategies for life and business. Her thought-provoking and practical approach gives participants ideas they can use immediately. Topics most requested are men and women at work, presentation skills, business etiquette, networking, leadership skills, and developing a winning personal style.

A past national president of the American Business Women's Association, Ann knows the issues that matter most to women. She brings the teaching style of a seasoned educator and over 20 years of experience in corporate management to her seminars. Ann connects to her audience through personal stories and a fun approach to learning. She provides customized workshops and keynotes for companies and conventions.

Ann holds a master's degree in education and has written for *HersKansas* and *Women in Business* magazines. Workshops available include:

- Don't Go Hunting Bears With a Stick
- Managing the Challenge of Change
- Making Waves – Developing Your Own Personal Style
- Let's Do Lunch!
- Can You Hear Me Now?

Ann E. Mah
Topeka, KS • 785-266-9434 • www.annmah.com

Ann E. Mah, M.S.

Oh Behave!

Etiquette essentials for women on the go

It's going to happen. Whether you are a stay-at-home mom or a business professional, you will find yourself in social situations wondering if you are doing the right thing. Perhaps you invited a local business leader to lunch to convince her to donate to your favorite charity. Now you're wondering how to handle the check. Do you pay? Do you split the bill?

Etiquette is not just a set of rules to be pulled out when you go to a banquet. It is not just a matter of using the right fork or sending a thank you note. Etiquette is using consideration when you deal with people. It means you have good people skills and you use them. Good etiquette shows that you pay attention to other people and are aware of their needs. The good news is that it is easy to learn and you can practice almost anywhere.

My favorite place to practice good etiquette is the local grocery store. I look people in the eye and smile. That may be the only smile some people get all day. I call the checkout people by their names. Everyone likes to hear her name used. It's common sense, it's useful every day, and it's something we can all learn. So let's get started.

Let's do lunch!

Everyone wonders how to handle etiquette when dining out. Inviting someone to lunch provides a good opportunity to get acquainted with a new friend or meet a client for the first time. However, situations occur that give pause to even the most seasoned executive. It is hard enough to focus on cutting the deal or making a good impression without worrying about your table manners. Knowing what to do in social situations gives you confidence. We are going to focus on the most common mistakes people make dining out, so that whether you are with clients or your church committee, you will be comfortable handling the details that make a positive difference.

First—be here now. Give your complete attention to the situation and to those with whom you are dining. Be on time; early is better. Turn off your cell phone. Waiting in the restaurant lobby is best; but if you have been seated at the table, do not order anything until your guest arrives. A table with half-empty glasses and crumbs is not very inviting.

First impressions are made quickly and last a long time, so don't blow it. It used to be expected that women would remain seated when men arrived, but no more. If seated, stand up to greet your dining partner. Offer your hand and give a firm handshake. Let your opening statement show your appreciation for the meeting. Use your guest's name. For example, "Thank you for meeting with me, Jane."

If there are several in attendance and introductions are in order, make a proper introduction. When introducing two people, say the name of the most important person first. Who is most important depends on whether it is a business lunch or a social lunch. In business, rank rules. Your supervisor's name would be said before someone of lower rank. You might say, "Mr. Boss, I'd like you to meet our new assistant, Ms. Smith." When introducing a customer to your colleagues, say your customer's name first. In strictly social situations, men are often introduced to women, saying the name of the woman first. Younger people are introduced to older people, saying the name of the older person first. Get the idea? You decide who is most important and take the lead in introductions. Others will appreciate that you know how to handle the situation and help them get through the awkward stage of getting acquainted.

Small talk is important. It is how you connect before getting down to business. Ask open-ended questions rather than "yes-no" questions. Be prepared to listen and learn. Making that personal connection will pay off later when you call to follow up. You can start the call with one of your small talk topics and go from there.

Expect the unexpected! Learn the rules of restaurant dining so you know how to handle the various situations that may arise. Here are some commonly asked questions:

I have been asked to lunch at a nice restaurant. What do I order so I know what price range is good for my host? If you are the guest and are not sure what price range to order, ask your host for a recommendation.

What do I do with my napkin if I need to leave the table? Place the napkin in your lap after everyone has been seated. The host should take the lead on this. If you need to leave during the meal, place the napkin on your chair seat. Your napkin goes folded to the right of your plate when you are finished eating.

Which glass and butter plate are mine? Plates and utensils can be confusing. Just remember that solids are to the left and liquids to the right of your plate. Your bread and salad plates will be left of your plate and drinking glasses to the right of your plate. With the utensils, you ordinarily work from the outside in. The dessert fork will be placed above the plate.

What do I do if I drop my fork? If you drop your fork, leave it on the floor and let the waiter know the next time he returns to the table. If you drop something messy on the floor, like a spoonful of gravy, let someone know right away so no one steps in it.

When do we start eating? How do I pass the common items? In a group setting, wait until all are served before you begin eating. If you are the one to start passing the common dishes (like rolls or butter), offer to the person on your left first, then pass to the right. Take butter and jelly from the serving dishes and place them on your butter plate, not directly on the bread. Butter your bread a small piece at a time and leave the knife on the butter plate.

What if I ate something that I shouldn't have? How do I get it out of my mouth gracefully? The rule is that food comes out the same way it went in. That is, if you put it in your mouth on a fork, it comes out on a fork. If you ate it with your hands, use your hands to remove it. Of course in a choking emergency, just get it out!

Where do I put my fork while I'm talking? When you stop eating to visit, place your knife across the top edge of your plate, with the blade facing you. Place your fork on the bottom right corner of your plate. Place your knife and fork across your plate to signal the waiter that you're finished.

What if I spill something on my dining partner? If you spill food on your dining partner, offer to pay to have the clothes cleaned.

Remember that eating is secondary to the business you're conducting. If something is wrong with the meal, deal with it without making a fuss. If you are the guest, do not call the waiter over. If you are the host, take care of any problems at the table, but make any requests when the waiter returns to the table.

Usually, whoever extends the invitation pays the check, so don't make a big deal out of it if your host pays. You can do the inviting next time. If you are sharing the bill in a group just split it evenly, even if you had less to eat than others in the group. Women are notorious for getting out their calculators and splitting hairs! Just to be safe, take extra money in case you need it.

Friendships and deals can be won or lost over a meal. Showing that you know the rules of fine dining means that you do your homework and puts you and everyone else at ease. Enjoy the experience—and let's do lunch!

Making the most of networking events –

Sooner or later you will be invited to a networking event. It may be a cocktail hour "meet and greet" for your business or a reception for the Junior League. Networking is important to both your personal and professional lives, but meeting new people can be intimidating. Let's talk about a few rules for networking events that will help you feel more comfortable and make your "net-work" better.

First, have a goal in mind for the event. Maybe your goal is to meet two new clients. Maybe you want to get some leads on a summer job for your son. Perhaps you need to connect with a business leader so you can call her next month to sponsor a community benefit auction. Whatever the event, know why you are going. Then you can determine if your time was well spent.

Next, give yourself permission to act like the host, and not like a guest. Look for those people along the side of the room who want to get involved but are too shy to make connections. Introduce them to people you know. Since you already know how to do introductions, this will be easy. The new person will appreciate the effort. When you introduce two people, tell them something about each other so they have a reason to start a conversation. For example, "Mr. Jones, this is Sally Smith. She is the new vice president at First America Bank. She works with the business loan department." Helping others make connections and putting them at ease will make you the one people are talking about—in a good way.

An important part of making introductions is shaking hands. Men don't always know if women want to shake hands, so do not be shy about extending your hand first. A proper handshake is one where you reach all the way to the web between the thumb and forefinger, clutch the other person's hand firmly, pump the hand a couple of times and release. Make eye contact and smile. It is an easy way to make a good first impression. Believe me, people remember and take notice of wimpy handshakes. Do your children a favor and teach them to shake hands in a confident manner. It is a skill they will use for life.

If drinks are involved, carry them in your left hand so that your right hand is free to shake hands. It is embarrassing to change hands, wipe off the water from the glass, and offer a wet hand to someone!

Have you ever had someone get right in your face to talk with you? It is uncomfortable when a casual acquaintance or a stranger is too close. In the United States, a good talking distance is about eighteen inches to three feet. Any closer is invading the other person's space, and any farther is too far to make a connection. If you want to join a conversation already going on, it is not hard to do. Stand near the edge of the group and listen. When there is an opportunity, comment on the topic they are discussing. The group will usually open up and let you in.

Learning names can be the hardest part of a networking event. The trick is to let people know your name in as many ways as possible—visually and audibly. Wear a name badge. We are a visual society. Wear it on your right side, as most people shake hands with their right hand and their eyes will automatically go up your arm to your name. Repeat your name. Anne Baber, a networking expert and co-author of *Great Connections*, calls this the Forrest Gump method. You remember: "Hi, I'm Forrest. Forrest Gump." Repetition helps others remember your name and helps you remember their names. Repeat back to yourself the other person's name when meeting someone new. "It's good to meet you, Nancy." Our minds are just like computers. The more ways you input information, the more likely you are to be able to access that information when you need it.

Finally, an important part of working a room is knowing when to leave a group and move on. If you find yourself in a situation where the contact is not going to be of any benefit to your goal, the person makes you uncomfortable, or you just want to meet more people, just excuse yourself and move on. Say something such as "I've enjoyed visiting with you. Please excuse me, I see someone I need to visit with tonight." It's as simple as that.

Networking effectively is a key ingredient to success in any walk of life. Networking events can be a fun and beneficial way to grow your network. Just use that common sense consideration and have fun.

Putting it all together –

Good etiquette is lacking in society today. In this fast-food, drive-through world, it is no wonder we have lost the art of fine dining. Show etiquette to others and model it for your children by taking just a little time to make people feel at ease and appreciated. It's everyday etiquette, so behave!

CHAPTER TEN

Your Life's Legacy
Leaving love and laughter in your wake

Susan Meyer-Miller

As an international speaker, Susan Miller has made friends and memories worldwide. She has trained and motivated a half-million people in eight countries, has authored four books, is a small business owner and an occasional business commentator on Fox News.

Susan is known for her strong family values and kindred spirit. She loves to laugh, loves to cook, and loves to throw a party! She believes the quality of our relationships determines the quality of our lives. In 1995, finding herself suffering from "frequent flier fallout," she regained life balance by taking her career into her own hands and starting SpeakerUSA. She has become "The Customizer," creating motivational training programs specifically geared to help clients meet their challenges head-on.

After earning a B.A. in Human Resources Management, Susan began her career in the restaurant business building and leading teams. Her motto is *"let's get the job done and still have fun!"* As Training Manager for the world's largest Pizza Hut franchise, she guided all levels of training for 450 restaurants, managed the corporate training center, and published the company newsletter. In 1990, Susan joined Fred Pryor Seminars as a speaker and began an eight-year adventure of travel, teaching, and discovery.

Today Susan is a wife, stepmother, and grandma. She is active in her community and was named 2002 Woman of the Year by her local American Business Women's Association chapter.

SpeakerUSA
Shawnee, KS • 877-674-8446 • www.speakerusa.com

Susan Meyer-Miller

Your Life's Legacy

Leaving love and laughter in your wake

> *History will be kind to me,*
> *for I intend to write it.*
>
> – Winston Churchill

Don't look now, but you are leaving a legacy!

You are leaving your spirit behind everywhere you go. Take care to live your life deliberately, knowing you are having an impact—no matter how small—on those around you. Your legacy is yours and yours alone. By definition, legacy means "passing on from generation to generation." Essentially, your actions and words leave an impression on those you meet, young and old, as you journey through life.

How do you wish to be remembered? What are you known for now? Who looks to you for guidance or support? Do you think consciously about how you influence others? What is *your* legacy? Some of us will prepare children to be amazing adults. Others will write books or make movies. But most of us will leave our legacies through the simple acts of daily living and the quality of our relationships. You don't have to be a parent to influence someone or spread a little love around. You don't have to be talented or famous, brainy or bold. You just have to be you.

In this chapter I've put together a short list of ideas to inspire you to live with purpose and to share your spirit with others. I hope it will spark your enthusiasm and serve as a reminder to live with love and to leave a wonderful legacy of lessons and laughter in your wake.

Making Meaningful Memories

At my father's funeral, my cousin Nancy said, "Uncle Marvin always asked you what you were up to. He made you feel important about what you were doing." I heard story after story about my father as people recounted memories of his life. He was gracious and made choices based on his family values. He said the things that mattered in the moment. His legacy of lessons, love and laughter inspires me to do the same.

People make meaningful memories every day. They celebrate traditions from the past or build new ones. They take time out to share their knowledge or to give encouragement. We remember the people who make good times better and bad ones easier. But life is busy, and it is easy to simply move about on a superficial level defining our success on other people's standards and getting caught up in the logistics of managing a family. Building *connected* relationships takes time. Slow down and cherish the moment, celebrate life, and bring meaning to what happens along the way. This is both our task and our reward.

Have Fun!

"When we think of you, we smile" was the epitaph chosen for our friend Kevin who slipped from us too soon, leaving a huge chasm in the lives of his friends and family. My friend Sue said in her eulogy, "When this man walked into the room, he lit it up. He was funny, gregarious, and wild. We loved that about him." Although Kevin was an adult and a father, he never lost his childlike sense of humor and play. When we were with him we were laughing and happy.

Don't save your fun for vacations and holidays; take time out to play right now. Skate with the kids. Have a family game night. Find the humor in frustration. Be silly and laugh out loud! It will do you good. Building fun and adventure into your life on a daily basis helps you to rejuvenate and, best of all, creates memories that last a lifetime.

Celebrate Important Life Events

Honor accomplishments and special milestones in your loved ones' lives. Attend their important events and celebrations. At a recent grade school graduation, I witnessed a young girl in the front row on stage searching the crowd. She wouldn't sit still, craning her neck and moving around, seeking the face she longed to see. For the next 20 minutes, I prayed she would find that face. Finally, a man entered the back door, windblown and in a hurry. When she saw him, she waved, mouthed "Hi, Dad," and immediately sat up, beaming from her place on stage. When her name was called, she walked proudly to get her diploma and again, looked into the crowd to be sure he was watching.

It was so important for the young girl to have her dad there on her special day. Be aware how your presence matters to others when they graduate, receive an honor, or celebrate a birthday. If you can't be there, send a card. But don't just sign it; include some of your *own words* to recognize the accomplishment.

Writer Raymond Aaron began a birthday tradition when his daughter, Juli-Ann, was born. Each year he starts a file with mementos and thoughts about the important events in Juli-Ann's life. He then writes a letter, places all the treasures with it, and seals them in an envelope, printing "Letter to Juli-Ann on her *nth* birthday. To be opened when she is 21." On her birthday, they go together to the bank and place it in the deposit box with the letters from past years. Sometimes she takes out the others and handles them. She is so looking forward to her 21st birthday. Aaron says, "It is a time capsule of love … a gift of loving memories from one generation to the next." What a great birthday present.

How do you honor your loved ones' special days and achievements? Can you think of creative ways to make the day important? Do you take time out of your busy schedule to be there? Sometimes, just being there makes all the difference.

Carry on Family Traditions

I never felt so disjointed as the time I spent Thanksgiving in Australia. Of course, they don't celebrate Thanksgiving there; it's an American holiday. But my family celebrates with the big dinner and Mom's gravy and maybe a game of Scrabble. You can count on it. Occasionally people will just drop in because they know we will be there. That year, after having a turkey croissant in the hotel restaurant, I called home to chat with everyone. Only five people had shown up at Mom's, and we were all a little sad. Traditions give us a sense of security and belonging. I vowed then that I would always be home for Thanksgiving. Now that she is weaker, suffering from illness, the preparations fall on me. I do it for her—and it's sometimes a struggle—but I do it *her* way. It is important to her and to the rest of the family.

As families blend we must be flexible about holiday traditions and not forget to include the elders. This can be a challenge. A friend once said, "Christmas is a nightmare! We take the kids first to my mother's, and then to my dad's. After that, we drop them at my ex-husband's mother's, and he takes them to see *his* dad the next day." That sounds like a bit much, but if you avoid making demands or being difficult about *your* tradition, a solution can be found. Keep the spirit of celebration in mind. Remember: if you exclude a family member who is difficult, you are teaching your children to cut people off rather than to find a way to get along. Live with love!

Gift Giving

When I was 18, a co-worker came in one day and gave me a gift. She said, "When I saw it, I said to myself, that has Susan's name written all over it!" She said she could never find just the right gift at the right time and this was my birthday present—whenever it was. I like the idea of giving *meaningful* gifts. It isn't important to spend a lot; it is more important to be thoughtful. In ritualized gift giving, as at Christmas where everyone rips into their gifts in frenzy, the gift often loses its meaning.

For years, I gave a friend a two-dollar blank journal for Christmas. She counted on it! Every year she would tear into the paper with relish and say, "I knew it! Thank you!" My friend Pat is so hard to buy for, I make him lasagna. He loves it! Often instead of giving my nephews and nieces material things, I give them my time. I do whatever they want to do for a specified time.

Pass it on

Pass on important heirlooms, talents and recipes to the next generation. I learned to make my famous lasagna from my college roommate's Italian grandmother. She was from the old country and arrived with two heavy bags. She had brought her pots and pans and all the food. She took over our kitchen and spent the next five hours teaching us how to make lasagna the "right way."

What special talents do you have to pass on to another? Is there a family recipe or special food you would like to teach your children to make? What about a family Bible or other book telling the story of your family? Take time to pass it on.

Perfect the Art of Storytelling

Storytelling is an ancient form of connection and memory. Stories carry our history and traditions, our values, and lessons for living. They give us courage and hope. Children love to hear stories about their families. They listen for clues about who they are and where they came from. Sadly, television has replaced the dinner table, and generations no longer live in the same home. This disconnect is eroding our roots and bringing about the sense of isolation we see so often. Healthy, respectful relationships are founded on people listening to, understanding, and knowing each other's stories.

Tell your stories to your kids and encourage older family members to talk about what it was like in their time. As people age, it becomes even more important for them to tell their stories—to relive their lives. Encourage children to tell *their* stories and to listen respectfully without interrupting or saying, "We know Dad, we've heard that story before." My nephew, Tyler, is a slow talker in a family of fast talkers. The others have to be told to calm down and let him tell his story in *his* way.

Create your own family living history by asking members to share their photos and memories. Have your children interview the older generation and then create a video or website to document that history. Help them plan the topics they are interested in and prepare questions in advance. Tip: remember to transfer your information periodically into a newer media format.

Family Vacations

Many Baby Boomers remember the annual family road trip with affection. My dad would take out the map, gather us around the table, and let us help decide where to go. For some reason, unbeknownst to me, my brother always wanted to go to Wichita. We would mark our destination, plot our route, and decide what stops to make on the journey. One year we stopped at every cowboy museum west of the Mississippi. We played "red car" and "I spy" to pass the time. We never did make it to Wichita!

Wherever you go, make memories along the way. It is not necessary to schedule every moment. Stressing out will not serve your purpose. Stop to see a sunset or take an interesting side road. Let family members each pick one thing they want to do and do it. Let them have some quiet time, too. Remember: the word recreation is re-creation.

Girl Trips

A friend shared that her mother always called the family vacation a "trip." She said it was not a vacation for her because she still had to carry out her duties—especially on camping trips. She insisted on vacationing with her sister, so she could relax.

Many women now take annual "girl trips" where they can get up when they're finished sleeping, read uninterrupted, or get a little "retail therapy!" They shed the roles of mom or wife and rekindle both their own energy and their relationships with friends. Could you use a break away from the many roles you play as a busy woman? Have you and a friend been saying for years that you'll have to get away together … but you never do? Plan your girl trip today, and then follow through.

Create a Photo Log

Make it a family project or just do it yourself, but organizing your photos can be a lot of fun. Set them up chronologically by era or event. For instance, you might have an album labeled "College," "Baby's First Year," or "Florida Vacation." You could gather the family around the table and have them create a scrapbook documenting a recent event. They could label the pictures and add funny captions and mementos they picked up along the way. Spending time together reliving the fun reinforces the laughter and joy, and it will multiply in the future when they share the scrapbook with their own kids.

Label your family pictures for future reference. At a recent family reunion my aunt produced an envelope of old photos. She wanted to write the names on the back of each picture. She, Mom and their cousins sat and reminisced while labeling each picture, but there were many they did not know. Don't wait to organize your photos. Do it now while those who have the knowledge are still with you.

Make New Friends, but Keep the Old …

…one is silver, and the other's gold. I remember this song from Girl Scouts and have tried to make it a practice throughout my life. One of the greatest joys in life is reminiscing with old friends. Friends remind us who we are when we have forgotten. Some friends are more like family than our real family. I'm pleased my family has passed on the legacy of maintaining old friendships and keeping traditions with them. Dad would celebrate the Fourth of July with his old football buddies, and they still visit Mom to see how she's doing.

My friend Kenda is the sister fate forgot to give me. She is part of my family; I am part of hers. After college we moved apart, but I refused to lose track of her. She always says, "I moved all over the country and couldn't get rid of her if I tried!" Now we have been through so much together—death, marriage, birth, and disagreements—and found our way through them. The secret is unconditional love. We are comforted knowing we will always be there for each other. The day of my wedding she said, *"You're my root."* That was the best gift she could give me.

Are you taking care of your friendships or taking them for granted? Is there someone you have lost touch with who would love to hear your voice? Do you have any fences to mend with old friends? Pick up the phone or drop a card in the mail and make a friend's day. Be the one to keep in touch even if you are the only one who does the calling. More importantly, don't give up your girlfriends when you marry or start a family.

Little Rituals

My father traveled for his job, and when he would leave for a trip he would give me a kiss for every day he was going to be gone. He would count each day on his fingers and give me a kiss. I'll never forget that. It made saying goodbye so much easier. Little rituals like this add meaning to life and connect us to one another.

One man told me his son would sit on the toilet every morning when he was shaving. For ten minutes or so he would ask questions and talk about school or his friends. The dad said sometimes he was thinking about work or in a hurry and would feel annoyed, but at around age nine, his son stopped coming, and he realized how much he missed it.

When my husband's father died, all the children went to his mother's home to be together and say goodbye. After the service, everyone went out to the back patio and my sister-in-law took out her scissors and cut Mother's hair. One by one, family members took a turn in the chair. I had the feeling this was a family ritual and seemed to bring comfort and connection in a time of grief.

My stepdaughters have fond memories of my husband cooking brunch for them on weekends. He made bacon, eggs and hash browns. Sometimes he would make waffles or pancakes. "It always took forever," they said, "but it was *sooo* worth it." On a recent visit they asked him to make breakfast. Everyone helped out and the food tasted like love.

Can you think of some little rituals performed by a family member or friend that meant something special to you? What rituals do you share that add meaning to life and give the feeling of security or belonging? Can you think of some new rituals to start with your family or friends that they will always remember?

Live Your Legacy

Think about your own memories. What are the defining moments of your life? Who made a difference to you, taught you lessons, or gave you encouragement? What traditions were practiced in your family or neighborhood? Who helped you turn things around when you were off track? It is the little things that count—the magical or encouraging comments that are the most memorable. How are you leaving your spirit behind in this life? What magical memories have you created? I hope reading this chapter inspired you to live deliberately and leave a little love and laughter in your wake.

Go! Live today like you'll remember it forever!

CHAPTER ELEVEN

Mental Makeover
Renovating the inches between your ears

Connie Michaelis

"Nothing is manifest on the outside that is not first manifest on the inside," says Connie Michaelis. The journey of personal growth is the journey to true success. Connie started her Mary Kay career 13 years ago and today is in the top 1% of the sales force nationwide. She is currently driving her sixth pink Cadillac and has taken trips around the world as a result of her sales efforts and team building. Connie says the real prize is the person she has become.

Connie received a B.A. in Education from the University of Kansas and taught secondary general science and biology. She raised four children and today has seven grandchildren (as we go to press). She spent ten years as a Lay Counselor and Pulpit Supply for the Presbyterian Church. She has served in numerous volunteer organizations and community service activities.

Connie's personal mission statement is to "face fear by faith and help others do the same." Her passion for empowering and enriching women's lives has given her opportunities to speak at conferences and workshops all over the United States. Mary Kay Cosmetics has become the positive environment for Connie's continued personal growth and life success. Connie may be reached by email at mkconnie@cox.net.

Connie Michaelis
Topeka, KS • 785-271-6804 • www.marykay.com/conniem

Connie Michaelis

Mental Makeover

Renovating the inches between your ears

Can you imagine being a few inches from crossing the finish line? Can you visualize being just inches from reaching the top of Mount Everest? Can you fathom being only inches from achieving your greatest goal?

The truth is that you are closer than you know to whatever you want in life. What may seem like an impossible journey is really a matter of a few inches. Those inches are the ones between your ears. Just for fun, put your hands up to your face, hold your head in your hands, and say, "I have the most powerful tool in the world right here between my hands!"

Although I have spent many years building a successful cosmetics business, I know that the most important makeover in a woman's life is a mental makeover. Sure there is power in changing appearance—we have all felt the impact of a bad hair day! The way we perceive our appearance directly affects how we feel about ourselves. Nevertheless, the most powerful makeover tool we have is the ability to makeover our minds.

Mary Kay Ash's son, Richard Rogers, says that Mary Kay Inc. is not primarily in the cosmetics business. Instead, Mary Kay is in the "people-building" business. How true that is, and how profound are the implications for every woman. We can do virtually anything that we "make up" our minds to do. The whole process of renovating our thinking patterns is very powerful. People can change outwardly if they can change inwardly! Every one of us has the ability to make major life changes by altering our thoughts and, consequently, our self-talk. Sometimes it truly is "all about me"! The battlefield of life is not "out there," somewhere apart from our true selves. It is "in here." The solution to so many of our problems lies in renovating our minds.

Libraries bulge with psychology and self-help books to assist us in working our way out of every kind of problem. But rather than waiting until we have time to study all those books, there are some *simple* ways to begin the mental makeover. Notice that I do not use the word *easy*, because that means no effort is required. *Simple* implies that everyone can participate. I use that word because what I am about to tell you is not complicated or hard to comprehend.

My friend Judy is the mother of an adult son with Down's Syndrome. Aaron always seems to be happy and have a positive outlook. With his innocent view of life he avoids the negative thought patterns that burden most adults. Aaron is uncomplicated. He has a simple and delightful attitude toward life. I would imagine that his thought patterns are healthy and his self-talk is positive. When he goes to work at a local restaurant to wash dishes, he finds little to complain about and gets along well with co-workers. Aaron believes that his work is important and that everyone likes him. Can you imagine what a difference it would make in the world if we all believed our work was important and everyone liked us?

Aaron inspires me to take the simple approach to a positive attitude. It is not your IQ that is the deciding factor, but your attitude, persistence, motivation, and self-talk. Every individual has the power to change her mind and, consequently, to change her life. It may not be easy, but it is simple.

Every day we choose whether to respond to our circumstances in negative or positive ways. Few of us recognize and practice using the power we have. We do not make conscious decisions about how we will respond. Instead, our emotions lead the way and dictate our responses. We simply react. An all-too-common example of a knee-jerk reaction comes when another driver cuts in front of us on the highway. We immediately become angry and lay on the horn—or worse. Of course, we have no idea what circumstances might have caused that person to be in such a hurry. Would we respond differently if we knew that the other car was on the way to the hospital in an emergency?

Poor driving is not the reason for our instant irritation; it is the sense that someone else invaded our space. Where does the anger come from? The inches between our ears are filled with messages that filter all events.

Genetics, upbringing, and life experiences combine to give us a worldview that colors how we interpret every situation. Negative thoughts and attitudes lock us into self-defeating patterns. Our minds need a makeover to learn new and healthy responses.

Wouldn't it be a relief to know that your primary responsibility in life is simply to manage the space between your ears? That the playing field of life is not your home, your job, your family, friends, or your area of influence? The fact is you are not in charge of acres of issues, or miles of concerns, or oceans of emotions. All you really need to worry about are just a few inches of grey matter. Instead of taking on the problems of the world, concern yourself with the inches between your ears. Imagine a picture of Atlas with his hands on the sides of his face, supporting only his own head, instead of carrying the Earth on his back. Whew! What a relief!

So it is with the mental makeover.

We need to quit looking for things to change on the outside. We need to quit blaming others and searching for excuses for our predicaments. This is the ultimate expression of personal responsibility. The mental makeover does not allow for victims. Take charge of the six inches between your ears.

How do you begin this mental makeover? By monitoring your inner dialogue. Be more self-aware. Your mind is filled with negative self-talk. We would never talk to another human being the way we talk to ourselves. Our mental tapes have messages that too often defeat us: "I feel insecure around other people." "I'm not as smart as my co-workers." "I'll never be as successful as I would like to be." As far as we know, human beings are the only animals that can talk to themselves. Scientists say that 85% of our waking time is spent in an internal dialogue. That is the good news and the bad. If the conversation is healthy, then the dialogue is beneficial. But if that inner dialogue is negative, the results are self-defeating.

Scripture encourages us to think on positive things. The Bible tells us that as a man thinks in his heart, so he is. Philippians 4:8 (NIV) says: "Whatever is true, whatever is noble, whatever is right, whatever is pure, whatever is lovely, whatever is admirable—if anything is excellent or praiseworthy—think about such things." Proverbs 17:22 (NIV) tells us: "A cheerful heart is good medicine, but a crushed spirit dries up the bones." One of my favorite encouragements toward healthy self-talk comes from Marianne Williamson in her book, *A Return to Love*:

Our deepest fear is not that we are inadequate.
Our deepest fear is that we are powerful beyond measure.
It is our light, not our darkness, that most frightens us.
We ask ourselves, who am I to be brilliant,
gorgeous, talented, fabulous?
Actually, who are you not to be? You are a child of God.
Your playing small does not serve the world.
There is nothing enlightened about shrinking so that
other people won't feel insecure around you.
We are all meant to shine, as children do.
We were born to make manifest the glory of God that is within us.
It is not just in some of us; it is in everyone.
And as we let our own light shine, we unconsciously
give other people permission to do the same.
As we are liberated from our own fear, our presence
automatically liberates others.

The most powerful way to reprogram your mind is to change your self-talk. Positive affirmations are the cosmetics of a mental makeover. It may be impossible to entirely remove negative self-talk, but it is entirely possible to superimpose new thoughts. Just like the beauty regimen for your face, the mental makeover needs daily applications of positive pronouncements and healthy self-talk, statements that improve the dialogue within. Self-talk creates new habits and healthy grey matter. Nido Qubein, a national speaker on business motivation, says the expression, "garbage in equals garbage out," is not correct. Rather, it is garbage in, garbage stays and gives birth to triplets! It is critical to overpower that negative garbage with life-giving thought patterns. The choice is yours: Live in a negative world or design and adopt daily positive affirmations.

The important thing is to immediately recognize the need for healthy self-talk and begin the makeover. As the Nike ads say, "Just Do It!" An excellent resource for this project is the best-selling book, *Secrets of Super Selling, How to Program Your Subconscious for Success.* In it, Lynea Corson and co-authors George Hadley and Carl Stevens describe a detailed reprogramming process. You may choose to begin by sitting down with pen and paper and conducting a personal analysis of your self-talk. Write down negative statements that course through your mind such as "I feel inadequate compared to other people." "I am disgusted when I look in the mirror." "I am afraid to make changes." Then, one by one, turn those statements around. For each one, write a contrasting statement, such as:

"I am on a personal journey of excellence. I do not compare myself to anyone."

"I do healthy things for myself daily. I am beautiful and I treat myself with kindness."

"I embrace every opportunity that comes my way. I am excited to see what comes next!"

The statements must be personal and present tense. It is important to keep a printed list of all the positive statements and repeat them daily, especially in times when the negative chatter starts.

If you don't have the time to do a great deal of personal introspection, you can jump-start the process by simply adopting the positive self-talk of people whom you admire and respect. The important thing is the repetition of positive words. David R. Hawkins, Ph.D., in his book *Power Vs. Force: The Hidden Determinants of Human Behavior,* emphasizes the importance of repetition. Coming from a purely scientific standpoint, Hawkins says: "...repetition of a slight variation over time results in a progressive change of pattern, the effect of the minute variations becomes amplified until it eventually affects the entire system and a new energy pattern evolves." Whether or not we understand why it works, we can simply enjoy the results. Daily repetition has a compounding effect, much like investing money. The results are not dramatic at first, but with time, it is life changing. Remember, it is not necessarily easy, but it is simple!

You may choose to begin by repeating passages from scripture, such as:

I can do all things through Christ who strengthens me.

(Phil. 4:13)

Or Dr. Norman Vincent Peale's favorite:

This is the day the Lord has made;
I will rejoice and be glad in it.

(Ps. 118:24)

Dr. Peale admonishes his readers to repeat it in a strong, clear voice and with positive tone and emphasis. Another source might be Emile Coué, a 19th century French professor who became a pioneer of affirmation techniques. It was believed that hundreds of patients in Europe and North America were cured by repeating the following affirmation each morning and evening:

Every day, in every way, I'm getting better and better.

Mary Kay Ash trained her sales force with the words:

Don't say I can't, I hope, I'll try. Say I can, I will, I must.

Another wonderful source of personal affirmations is Dr. Wayne Dyer, best-selling author and speaker. Dr. Dyer has spent years training people to excel in their personal and professional lives. He writes about seven primary attributes of healthy people in his book, *The Power of Intention.* He suggests our daily mantra should be:

*I am creative, kind, loving, beautiful, ever expanding,
endlessly abundant, always receptive.*

One of the most powerful books ever written on this subject is *Man's Search for Meaning,* by Viktor Frankl. Frankl was a Jewish psychiatrist imprisoned in a German concentration camp during World War II. He was stripped of all possessions and suffered three years in the most horrible and degrading of circumstances. He was among the few who survived the Holocaust. In his immediate family all but one sister was murdered.

Liberated at the end of the war, Frankl lived to write several books and developed a form of treatment for psychological problems called Logotherapy. The basis of the treatment is capturing the power of your own mind. While in the prison camp, Frankl had a revelation: His thoughts and the attitudes he chose to exhibit were the only parts of his life over which his captors had no power. They took everything else away from him. They even took the fat off of his body. But they could not control his mind. Frankl used the power within those few inches that his captors could not touch to not just survive, but to become an empowered human being. His life's work became helping others to do the same.

Frankl reminds us that even though we may have tragic circumstances in our lives, we have no excuse not to train our minds to focus on the positive. Keep in mind, the mental makeover is not necessarily easy because it requires effort and diligence, but it is simple and available to everyone no matter what their life situation. If Viktor Frankl could survive a concentration camp and manage to keep a healthy attitude, then none of us can reasonably claim that our circumstances are impossible.

As you design your personal affirmations, tape them on the bathroom mirror, the steering wheel of your car, and on your desk—and repeat them. The mental makeover begins with a three-times-a-day "beauty" prescription. As you repeat the positive statements, you reprogram your brain to act on those thoughts. It is as if you have a new filter in your mind. Your responses are changed. The negative filter is gone and a new one unfettered by past experience is put into place. Continuing the "beauty prescription" analogy, it is like cleaning the dirt and debris from your face and adding all new beautiful color. A transformation occurs. Soon, the woman looking into the mirror will see the visible results of her mental makeover!

Remember, your aspirations and the goals you set are fulfilled first in your mind. You are only six inches away from the desires of your heart. My personal affirmation is below. Feel free to make it your own. Begin your mental makeover today!

I am great and because I am great,
great things happen to me.
I am powerful and because I am powerful,
I can do anything right here and right now.
I am love and because I am love, people are drawn to me
and I love them unconditionally.
I am faithful and because I am full of faith,
fear has no place in me.
I am rich and because I am rich,
I have choices to make and gifts to give.

Personal Affirmations

CHAPTER TWELVE

From Life Transition to Transcendent Power
Five tactics to survival, esteem, and success

Debra Neal, LPC

Debra Neal, president of Pathways to Empowerment, is a trainer, motivational speaker, and therapist with over 17 years of experience in behavioral health. Debra brings fresh dimensions of teamwork and leadership excellence, diversity competence, and workplace wellness to corporate, educational, and governmental organizations.

An award-winning member of Toastmasters International, Debra captivates, entertains, and energizes as she educates her audiences. Debra's most requested keynotes include "Five Sacred Principles to Living a Satisfying, Serene, and Successful Life," "Middle Age: The Sweet Center of Life," and "Bring Out the Best in You."

A Licensed Professional Counselor, her private practice includes working with individuals and couples who are tired of living with addictions and compulsive disorders, unsatisfying relationships, and mood disorders that cloud day-to-day functioning.

Her chapter, a "must read," lends a fresh view about life transitions common to us all. It has been said that there are only three musts: we must die, must pay taxes, and must endure never-ending change and transition. This chapter provides you with a practical and empowering roadmap through change and transition to a new level of excellence in living.

Pathways to Empowerment
Lenexa, KS • 816-805-0732 • www.pathwaystoempowerment.net

Debra Neal, LPC

From Life Transition to Transcendent Power

Five tactics to survival, esteem, and success

About two months ago I went to a local community college production of the acclaimed post-Civil War drama *Flyin' West*, about the life of African American matriarch Sophie Leah and her family. From her home in Memphis, Tennessee, Sophie moved West to settle in an all black township, Nicodemus, Kansas. Many of her family and friends chose to remain in their familiar yet racist and poverty-stricken community. Moving West brought great promise of free land, economic prosperity, humanity and racial equality. Sophie took her possessions and her fears and pioneered West.

After years of arduous work and living in the throes of Jim Crow segregationist laws, she became a homeowner and farmer-entrepreneur, as well as a political and social advocate. Sophie built an empire and handled whatever daunting life challenges came her way.

The heroine of the play turned out to be my personal hero in the truest sense. She trusted in the unchartered journey West. She believed that her future beheld something infinitely greater than what was before her.

Walking through life transitions is inevitable and unavoidable. It has been said that we are always on the verge of, in the midst of, or just coming out of a major life-changing circumstance. In this chapter we focus on the promises that come with life transition and learn about barriers that may surface as we navigate through transition phases. Moreover, we take an up close and captivating look at five tactics that take you through a life change to a transcendent life experience.

Unlike Sophie, many of us would rather remain in a current circumstance, however threatening, painful, and dissatisfying, than to squarely face that which is uncertain and unknown.

Wouldn't you agree that we as women seek order, rhythm, synergy, and structure? Changing a long-standing family holiday tradition, taking a different route to work, or trying a new hairstyle are small but difficult measures of change that we consequently meet with fist-folded resistance. Change is uncomfortable and we don't like it! To what measures have you ever gone to avoid making a change decision?

You can think of change as a discrete event, decision, or action. Transition, however, is the process of dealing with or the response to change. For instance, Mary has been given a new job responsibility (change). Her response ("I don't like this new job. I am not familiar these new duties. I am worried that I won't do well.") is the transition and reflects how she handles herself through the change.

I have been through two major transitions in my lifetime. The first came with divorce after 10 years of marriage. How about this for a book title: *From a Decade of Marriage With No Children to Divorce and Single Parent in Two Years: The Scariest Thing That Ever Happened.* I awoke one morning to find myself separated and raising my newborn alone. I had never felt so lost, alone, and frightened in all of my life. Being a first-time mother and caring for a newborn felt awkward rather than instinctive. The anxiety was more than I could stand on some days. I felt as clumsy as a football player taking ballet. It truly was a dark moment.

The second darkest moment came when I started having performance issues on my job. Perimenopause brought symptoms causing poor judgment, difficulty in concentration, tardiness, conflict with co-workers, and self-doubt—all of which affected my sense of worth and competence. I lived in fear of losing my job. The more I tried to improve, the worse things seemed to get. My greatest fear came to pass. I was terminated.

It wasn't as horrible as I had feared. The company terminated my position along with five others' full-time positions. So I was not alone. We were told it was due to loss of major revenue sources over the past year since 9-11. It turned out to be one of the best gifts I ever received.

Be it a "we regretfully inform you that your services are no longer needed," "I fell out of love with you a long time ago, and I don't want to be with you," the unanticipated death of family member, or a debilitating health problem, we all face *big* life changes. Life seems to stay on the same course for a while and then it takes a sharp turn downhill, uphill, and upside-down. It reminds me of a slow-motion roller coaster ride.

Let's take an up close and personal look at commonplace responses to change. Our problem solving techniques can be a bridge or a barrier. We will first examine the barriers.

The Panic Factor –

Did you grow up with a "be careful" message? I have heard the words "be careful" a thousand times during my life. As far back as my middle school years, every time I left home I heard, "Be careful!" One day my 16-year-old daughter, who had been driving (with license, insurance, and constant admonitions), was leaving for school. As I walked her to the car, I heard myself say, "Be careful." Though I had delivered that rote and unconscious admonition at least a hundred times, the light bulb went on. I realized that I had issued an ominous verdict underneath those words: be careful … don't take risks … watch yourself … proceed with caution.

It's no wonder that as we drive on the road of life proceeding with watchfulness and prudence that we panic when the road suddenly takes a sharp right turn. It is just like the rollercoaster, except there is no joy in the ride. Another reason feelings of panic overtake us is that we have the mistaken belief that if we are driving along the rode slowly enough that we can see what is before us clearly and navigate the drive perfectly. To our surprise, when the road is foggy or the view is blocked, terror sets in. We lack sufficient self-trust (I believe I can handle this) or self-efficacy (I have life skills that will equip) to handle the difficult road ahead. We prefer a road that is straight and smoothly paved, with no detours. When the road is curved, switched-backed, or uphill, road panic steps in.

The Control Factor –

I am sure you can relate to this one! We are impressed at our ability to plan, control, and manipulate circumstances, people, and events. We want to control how the family washes the dishes, how a co-worker completes the project, or when our boyfriend asks us to marry. For example, a wife may know how to get her husband to do that job he has been putting off.

Years ago in my married life, I bugged my husband for a year to paint the bathroom. I decided the situation could use some innocent manipulation. Pretend like you are going to paint the room yourself, I thought. I purchased the paint, set up to start, and it worked. I gambled that he would think that I would mess up the room. Wanting to be in control, he took over the job. The bet paid off and I felt in control. For every one attempt at control that works, fifteen other attempts fail. The degree to which we are attached to our own way of thinking is proportional to the degree of pain we experience when we face those major transitions that are beyond maneuvering.

The Gremlin Factor –

In the book *Co-Active Coaching Relationships,* by Laura Whitworth, Henry Kimsey-House and Phil Sandahl, the authors refer to "The Gremlin Effect." This is a self-limiting, self-defeating, and self-sabotaging thought pattern that surfaces when we are trying to make positive changes. The Gremlin Effect is an internal voice that causes one to feel paralyzed, frozen, or unable to move forward with productive transition actions. This slump can be the sabotaging work of the Gremlin—that inner voice that abhors change and demands the status quo: this is stupid ... too risky ... you're not ready ... you're not equipped. As soon as the Gremlin catches a whiff of significant life change, it is likely to show up in the form of thoughts that give us all the reasons why we should *not* change. The Gremlin is ever present and can effectively delay, frustrate, or create unnecessary pain in your transition experience.

Indecision Factor –

G. Ray Funkhouser's book, *The Power of Persuasion: A Guide to Moving Ahead in Business and Life*, talks about the relationship between uncertainty and lack of decision making. The greater the uncertainty about how a circumstance will play out, the greater the probability that an individual will live in an undecided state of mind. The greater the indecisiveness, the less likely the individual is to take action. In more extreme cases, indecision and uncertainty reveal themselves as a state of stagnancy or paralysis. Living in a state of indecision creates unwarranted anxiety and stress. Unbridled stress and anxiety cause sleep disturbance, poor appetite or overeating, fatigue, headaches, and stomachaches. They can also exacerbate other physical ailments.

Go back to a time in your life in the last five years when you felt indecision and uncertainty. Do you recall how this affected your body, your ability to think, and your sensibilities? Did you feel any sense of stagnancy or paralysis? Indecision takes a major toll on mind, body, and spirit. It profoundly affects our ability to transition effectively.

There is an art to transitioning through life. Women today have a wealth of roadmaps and clearly marked pathways to help us through. Like a clearly lit airport runway at night, there are resources that empower, equip, and propel us through life-changing events. These tools avail us of the chance to not only transition unscathed, but to be transformed and then transcend to a new level of empowerment, confidence, and a sense of "I will be OK." Here is a five-step tactic to help.

Tactic One: Upgrade Your Perception

Underneath the universal fear of change is the distorted belief that change is bad, negative, or something to be shunned. Many people believe change means things will never be the same, or if things change, they won't be as good, or that things are fine the way they are. Take a moment and ponder what change means to you.

Be creative and optimistic as you rethink what you want change or transition to mean for you. A glass that is half-filled can be thought of as "I have half the beverage left to *enjoy*" or "I *only* have half of the beverage left." What if we adopted a healthier perspective of that job loss or involuntary job relocation or other life transition? You might say to yourself:

- *It is scary, but it's okay.*
- *With help and support I can make this work.*
- *Out of the seed of adversity comes a seed of equal benefit.*
- *I can't see very far into the future and that is a good thing.*
- *I don't know how this will turn out, but I can make it work.*
- *Inch by inch anything is a cinch. Yard by yard anything is hard.*

Transformation of your thoughts leads to a transformation of your life. Tactic one helps overcome the Panic Factor and the Gremlin Factor—turning those Gremlin voices and the Panic voices into voices of power.

Tactic Two: Look for the Lesson

In the book *If Life is a Game, These are the Rules*, Cherie Carter-Scott, Ph.D., writes, "We are enrolled in a full time informal school called 'life.' Each day in this school you will have the opportunity to learn lessons. You may not like the lessons, but you have designed them as part of your curriculum." If you believe in your own personal higher calling, then you can welcome and greet significant life situations with open arms.

Our experiences are our lessons and our lessons are our experiences, and they lead us closer to reaching our authentic purpose, however painstaking. Believe that with the new comes new beginnings and new opportunities. Accepting this fact and looking for the *lesson* helps you to overcome the Indecision Factor.

Tactic Three: Eat the Elephant One Piece at a Time

My 16-year-old daughter decided to participate in a national oration competition that awarded $5,000 to the first place winner. The contestants would have to successfully compete on a local, state, and regional level in order to be eligible for the national competition. The hurdles involved: a) determining the feasibility of traveling to the regional competition site (three states away); b) writing the essay in the midst of a demanding academic and extra curricular schedule; and c) memorizing the speech. A conscious choice was made to take one step at a time—write the essay, memorize the speech, practice the oration, win the state contest, and then decide about competing on the regional level.

Four days before the state competition, the state judging coordinator could not locate qualified judges. The fight in me (and the strong desire to have $5,000 of financial assistance for college) would not allow this goal to be so abruptly defeated. Twenty-five long distance calls later, and with an eating the elephant a bit at a time mindset, I found three qualified judges and one alternate. Taking one bite of the elephant at a time works well in overcoming the Fear Factor, the Indecision Factor, and the Gremlin Factor. By the way, my daughter won the state contest, had a great win on the regional level, and is now going to the national competition.

Tactic Four: Get Help

Women are labeled as "super-woman, wonder-woman, and all-woman," able to juggle house, job, career, parenting, volunteer activities, etc. Some would even say that women possess an anti-dependent mindset: I can do it by myself. I don't need help. These beliefs do not support the transition process. Trying to handle a major loss, change, or personal crisis alone creates a profound sense of isolation. The tendency is to become less engaged in social outlets, less connected to others, and less motivated to do so. Of course, this is not true across the board. Some women have great support systems and relationships that are affirming and validating.

Having someone say, "You can get through this, Carol," or "I can help you with this, Morgan," or "Debra, this is hard but this too shall pass" comforts the soul. Find a mentor, personal coach, or sponsor. Establish and nurture relationships with other women that will help you get through your transition and transcend to a new level of excellence. During my first life crisis (divorce), I joined a weekly support group. Having a family with which I maintained telephone contact also helped tremendously. Seeking the help of a mentor, personal coach, or professional counselor is an effective way to overcome the Panic Factor, the Indecision Factor, or the Gremlin Factor.

Tactic Five: Laugh, Play, and Do
Those Things That Add Joy Every Day

Walking through a crisis or major transition can have a significant impact on emotions and make it difficult to function. It is not uncommon for women to experience some form of depression. Depression can range from mild to serious and can vary in the degree to which it compromises daily functioning. Symptoms of Major Depression include long-term sleep disturbance, appetite changes, decreased motivation and energy, irritability and thought disturbance. Heightened stress levels combined with a depressive mood make it difficult to make timely, constructive, and rational decisions. Even mild forms of depression make day-to-day living feel like walking uphill.

Instead:

- Find something to laugh at every day.
- Go out of your way to watch comedy movies.
- Read humorous books and articles.
- Look on the Internet for jokes and inspirational quotes.
- Take a half-hour to one hour per week to play ... play with your kids.
- Do something out of the ordinary, perhaps something that seems silly.
- Go dancing or take a dance class.

I have never met a woman who went salsa dancing who did not think it was a total blast. Have a ladies night out and go salsa dancing. Exercise is one of the most effective antidepressant and anti-anxiety medications you can take. It works wonders to increase energy, improve sleep and concentration, and contributes to a sense of emotional well-being. Paying attention to and strengthening your innermost self through laughter, play, and exercise during a transition period is worth its weight in gold. It is an investment that is guaranteed to give you power in each step of your transition journey.

Life transitions are inevitable and unavoidable. They can be uncomfortable, scary, and painful, but they can also bring tremendous opportunity for personal enrichment. As women, we have inherent resistances that create serious barriers to coping with life change. This chapter has provided five tactics that are practical, powerful, and transformational.

Life is about the shedding of the old and growing into the new. Like a caterpillar whose metamorphosis brings a brilliantly beautiful butterfly, life transition has always taken me to higher platform of self-awareness, self-efficacy, trust and reliance on God. It brings us closer to our higher purpose and to being viable agents to better serve our families and to contribute to our communities and our country. Transition brings us closer in touch with our authentic self-love, liking who we are, and the ultimate unconditional self-acceptance. Like my heroine Sophie, you can get to the other side—transitioned, transformed and transcended to a new level of excellence in living.

CHAPTER THIRTEEN

I Am My Own Warm-up Band
Living life as a bodacious woman

Jae Pierce-Baba

Jae Pierce-Baba is a woman who has made it her mission in life to encourage others to Lighten Up in both personal and professional settings. Jae believes that laughing, humor and a sense of fun and wonderment give you an edge in life. Jae believes that a sense of humor is an essential life skill. She is both personally enriching and professionally practical in her presentations.

Jae is founder and CEO of LipShtick Productions and a nationally recognized professional speaker, pediatric occupational therapist, comedienne, stage performer, published writer, wife and mother.

Jae recently was published in the book *Fantastic Customer Service: Inside and Out*. Jae blends wit, compassion, and knowledge in her keynotes and seminars so that audiences leave with a smile on their faces, a good feeling in their hearts and a clear understanding of how to bring humor into their lives on a daily basis.

LipShtick Productions
Wichita, KS • 316-946-0422 • www.jaepierce-baba.com

Jae Pierce-Baba

I Am My Own Warm-up Band
Living life as a bodacious woman

To someone passing in the hallway, the sounds of laughter, giggling, and mayhem coming from the general vicinity of the triple-locked door sounded almost hysterical. The source of the hubbub was me—trapped behind a steel and mesh door on a locked down psychiatric unit.

It had all started with that nerdy little man, the one who had gotten me on this state hospital ward in the first place. How had it come to this? I was a young adult, newly graduated from college as an occupational therapist and on my own in a strange town. I wasn't here at the state hospital by a court order. In fact, I was a newly hired but valued employee—the only one who could calm the nerdy little man when he was highly agitated.

Job done, I headed back to my office but had no keys to unlock the door. Losing my keys had taken on a whole new meaning, and I was feeling hostile emotions coming from some of the aggressive mentally ill patients. I desperately scanned the hall to find someone to spring me from the drama developing around me.

I was drawing a curious crowd of people to my immediate area. The patients were increasingly nervous. The facial expressions directed at me were full of alarm and apprehension.

Shaped by structure and their rigid, daily timed activities, these people were aware that this type of incident was not usual, not normal. The tension was getting high, the patients wondering how the inexperienced, naive, and new occupational therapist would handle this situation. What was I to do?

I BECAME BODACIOUS! To the utter amazement of my captive audience, I pulled out my sense of humor and I started doing the "roller coaster wave." The people appeared entranced, with quizzical looks on their faces as both my arms reached skyward and then to the ground while I was laughing and giggling.

My predicament was quite humorous to those gathered by the door and slowly the patients laughed and some joined me in the wave. The laughter drew people out of their offices and, as the door was unlocked, I smiled brightly, bowed slightly and went back to my office.

In the months following the episode, a gruff older gentleman would spot me and start doing the roller coaster wave with his arms and smile a toothy grin from ear to ear. He and I had connected in humor and, to me, it felt like an atmosphere of hope.

By using a solution that was humorous, unexpected and creative, I had made a powerful point in dealing with the problem. Instead of having an angry confrontation, I was determined to make fun of my situation, be bodacious in my attitude, and hope for a peaceful ending.

Everywhere I look I see potential Bodacious Women—women who are ready to break free from their "life must be so serious" selves and become aware of who they are and what they want in life. Are you asking yourself at this very moment: Am *I* a Bodacious Woman? What in the heck does bodacious mean? Will I get kicked out of the PTA if I admit I am a Bodacious Woman? Every woman holds a vision of herself, and her bodacious traits will reflect that vision. I applaud the women who do not let the process of living distract them from the changes they want to make for themselves.

Being bodacious is being a blend of bold and audacious daring, but this definition is not a one-size-fits-all for every woman. Women are individuals and their bodacious traits will be as varied as they are. Wearing a big brooch or funny socks may be the bodacious limit for some while others might buy the latest sports car. Celebrate your own unique and bodacious style and be proud of it.

Taking Bodacious Back to the Basics: The Virtues of a Bodacious Woman

<u>B</u>: *Be in the present.*

Yesterday is history, tomorrow is a mystery, but today is a gift and that is why we call it the present. Today, don't try to do ten things at once. Do just one thing at a time and give it your full attention. You will be amazed at how much you get done. You only have *now*—choose to be happy in the present moment! The question Bodacious Women need to ask themselves is not "How busy am I?" but, "What am I busy doing?"

I'll be happy when I get through school. I will be happy when I buy a house. I will be happy when…. Are you putting off happy until some time in the future? The thing about being happy is that you are greatly involved with the present. Decide to be happy every day on the journey, not just at the destination. Be appreciative of what you have and live in the present.

O: *Own your problems.*

Get over it. Bad things happen—even to Bodacious Women! Don't beat yourself up or consider yourself stupid or unworthy. A Bodacious Woman is slow to place blame and is willing to look at her own participation in a problem. People generally are surprised when they do something stupid, but mistakes are a part of life. If the mistake has you feeling mortified and embarrassed, just look at the comedic potential of the situation. Never underestimate the laugh out loud humor of sharing your blunders, funny stuff, and mix-ups with others. Poking fun at yourself helps you accept these unanticipated events. Start small and laugh at the minor things, then work up to the major ones. (NOTE: do *not* put yourself down.) *Blessed are the flexible, for they shall not be bent out of shape.*

D: *Don't take it personally.*

Cultivate an attitude of healthy detachment. Bodacious Women understand when a situation is truly "not their problem." A Bodacious Woman does not put up with abuse—verbal, mental or physical—by others in personal or business situations.

A: *Attitude.*

Joy is not in things; it is in us.

– Ben Franklin

The ability to lighten up is a state of mind and a positive attitude is a conscious choice. Choosing a positive attitude is a powerful decision. Surround yourself with people who make you feel good about the way you are and support your decisions in life.

Sometimes depression is valued—when a co-worker is down and depressed, everyone is worried. A happy, perky woman comes in whistling and everyone says, "What's she on?" Happy people attract happy people and negative people appear arrogant, superior, and distant. What attitude are you wearing?

<u>C</u>: *Competition, change, and creativity.*

Embrace competition. Putting other people at ease will get you further than intimidating them. *You don't have to blow out my candle to make yours burn brighter.*

Embrace change. Times change and old solutions are no longer the answers to new problems. Break free of the routine by cultivating the unexpected in your life. *One way to have a clean mind is to change it once in a while.*

Embrace creativity. New solutions increase creativity through new answers, new challenges and new ideas.

> *Imagination is more important than knowledge.*
>> – Einstein

> *Imagination rules the world.*
>> – Disraeli

<u>I</u>: *Invest in moments of magic and serendipity.*

Serendipity suggests that something fortunate happened out of the blue. You don't know where it came from, but there it is. Wonderful gifts and memories are created in uncontrollable and unpredictable circumstances, but are traceable to a series of events. Problems or disappointments can be turned into delightful opportunities days, years, and even decades later. Bodacious Women know and trust this phenomenon and keep their eyes open for serendipity.

<u>O</u>: *Be outrageous.*

Bodacious Women develop outrageous habits to entertain themselves. Think of two outrageous things you could do this week on or off the job. Some ideas:

- Face the rear in an elevator.
- Wear goofy glasses while driving.
- Pay your Visa with your MasterCard.
- Get some friends to all stare up and point while waiting in line.
- Do facial aerobics with your mouth and eyebrows at every stoplight.
- Turn the radio up loud. Put two tennis balls into a tube sock, tie it up, and tuck it behind your back while driving for an exquisite and cheap back massage.

As adults, we can always find something to occupy our time—something that needs to be done at work or around the house—and we forget to have fun. *We are our own entertainment center*; the responsibility for self-renewal lies within us. Bodacious Women know the importance of having laughter and humor in life and take that commitment seriously.

U: *Utilize relationships and networks.*

Bodacious Women cultivate relationships for various reasons and value deep, nourishing, long-standing friendships, as well as community networks for practical, day-to-day support. Bodacious Women seek out guides and mentors and make it their business to know other ambitious, talented and fun women. A Bodacious Woman is *never* happy inside the box. She would rather create her own universe and selectively let other Bodacious Women into it—no reason to invite people in that drag you down. Bodacious Women know that if they spend time with miserable people, they get what they deserve. Discover at least one person who brings out the best in you. From this friendship, many more will follow.

S: *Sassy.*

Sassy women are mischievous, full of fun, feisty, playful, impertinent, and lively. Bodacious and sassy women make a pursuit of happiness top priority in their lives.

She Who Laughs, Lasts

Bodacious Women have a good sense of humor. Laughter is free, legal, and has no calories, no cholesterol, no preservatives, no carcinogens and is easily accessible. Laughter is a healing power available to everyone. There is no hierarchy in humor—no one "gets" a joke better than someone else. What makes you laugh is unique to you and your special brand of humor receptors. The reality is that we don't work at putting humor in our lives, believing that humor is spontaneous. We sit around and hope something funny happens. You may not even remember the last time you had a good laugh. Getting into the humor habit and seeing the lighter side of life is life changing.

> *I realize that humor isn't for everyone—it's only for*
> *people who want to have fun, enjoy life, and feel alive.*
>
> – Ann Schaef

Laughter really is the best medicine and I know that when the government finds out how good it is for you, they *will* regulate it—so stock up. Humor is essential to our emotional well-being. Laughter discharges tension from the primary emotions of depression, fear, anger, and anxiety. It also is considered a mature coping strategy.

Laughter plays a surprisingly important role in our physical health. The physical act of laughter works muscles all over the body, doubles the pulse rate, and contracts the abdominal muscles. One laugh burns six calories. Arteries expand and contract, the endocrine system secretes hormones associated with alertness, and it is an incredible muscle tension reliever. Dr. William Fry, M.D., states that laughter is like "inner jogging" and believes that laughter throughout the day adds up as physical exercise. Fitness experts have determined that 20 seconds of hearty laughter is the cardiovascular equivalent of three minutes of strenuous rowing. WOW! That is a hard choice: rowing on a machine at the YMCA or sitting on my couch laughing at sitcom television.

Becoming more playful is the only way to overcome "Terminal Seriousness." Playfulness provides the basic foundation for your sense of humor but adults sometime forget how to have fun. Use a child as a fun mentor! An average four-year-old child laughs or smiles 300 to 500 times a day; an average adult laughs or smiles 15 to 17 times a day. Do the math and that means that we lose around 385 laughs a day between childhood and adulthood, and that is serious!

Society values a sense of humor. It is consistently ranked as one of the top five characteristics that people look for in a significant other, an employee, or a friend. Humor is a powerful social and business sales tool, setting you apart from the competition. Education, parenting, health care, corporations—all would benefit from the effects of lightening up.

> *Realize that a sense of humor is deeper than laughter,*
> *more satisfying than comedy and delivers more rewards than*
> *merely being entertaining. A sense of humor sees the fun*
> *in everyday experiences. It is more important to have fun*
> *than it is to be funny.*
> – Laurence J. Peter and Bill Dana

One of the best uses of humor is as a "stress buster." Research supports that laughter is a natural tranquilizer without side effects. "Stressed Is Dessert Spelled Backwards" is a life philosophy that the women of the world could benefit from. Find humor in the midst of stress by keeping funny props or toys such as Groucho glasses, rubber chickens, wax lips, or funny hats nearby in case of emergency. Because I am such good business-woman, I carry my comedy props in an expensive woven basket – so I can deduct it!

According to several studies, humor can set the stage for creative awareness and freeing of the mind. For instance, at Cornell University, students were given a problem to solve that was irrational. Those that had watched a comedy film before doing the task scored higher on the problem. Housework has always seemed irrational to me, which must be the reason I love laughing. I have an old weather-beaten sign in my kitchen that has a powerful word painted on it: Giggle. And when my eyes land on that word, I do.

Never Underestimate the Power of Bodacious Women Uniting!

My fun experience at the state hospital taught me how being a Bodacious Woman could open all sorts of interesting doors in life. All women are in a unique position to bring a new and fresh perspective to the "business-as-usual" world. Women are challenged daily to be true to them-selves in business, parenting, household management, etc. There is no end to the ways women make an impact on the world around them. Many women have lost touch with laughing out loud and how important laughter is in life. Do we need a total life change or do we simply need to put more spontaneous fun in our lives? Go forth, Bodacious Women, armed with your sense of humor and use it as a creative force, a communication tool and a team builder.

I celebrated my half-century on the planet by doing my infamous back flip off of our local swim club's high dive … in a vintage ball gown.

Now that's what I call being BODACIOUS!

CHAPTER FOURTEEN

Using the PMS™ Formula to Achieve Your Life's Goals

Heidi Richards, M.S., CLL, CPPM

Heidi Richards specializes in Helping Small Businesses Bloom™ by sharing her insights and experiences in leadership development, marketing and strategic planning—not to mention having FUN!

Her experiences in "growing" successful businesses and community organizations give her a greater perspective on the challenges companies and organizations face today, which she portrays through her seminars, retreats and the several books she has written.

In 1997 the American Business Women's Association named her a Top Ten Business Woman in America and in 2004 Heidi was inducted into the Broward County Women's Hall of Fame—just two of the dozens of awards Heidi has received in her almost 30 years as a business owner in South Florida.

Heidi considers herself an Elan'trepreneur™—a creative visionary, a business person others look to and emulate, one who mentors others in business. Her company, Eden Florist & Gift Baskets, was named Best Florist in Southwest Broward by readers of the *Miami Herald* for six years. Channel 7 WSVN named her one of three Best Florists in South Florida. She is also a facilitator for retreats, Mistress of Ceremonies for organizations of all sizes, a mentor to several small business owners and a contributing writer to dozens of publications including *The PMS Principles*™, a regular column she writes for *Balance Magazine*. She is the founder/cofounder of dozens of civic and professional organizations including The Women's ECommerce Association, International, Inc.

Heidi Richards, M.S., CLL, CPPM
Miramar, FL • 800-066-3336 • www.heidirichards.com

Heidi Richards, M.S., CLL, CPPM

Using The PMS™ Formula to Achieve Your Life's Goals

The purpose of goals is to focus our attention. The mind will not reach toward achievement until it has clear objectives. The magic begins when we set goals. It is then that the switch is turned on, the current begins to flow, and the power to accomplish becomes a reality.

– The Best of Success by Career Press

Goals Power Our Lives

For as long as I can remember, goal setting has been the driving force in my existence. The challenge of achievement motivates me to work hard, dream big, learn all I can, and never give up. It is what "powers my life." How about you? If you are reading this book, you are a person who has already realized goals, or who wants to and just needs a little guidance. There are many benefits to setting and achieving goals. The obvious include having a feeling of accomplishment, stretching your capabilities, and getting what you want. Goal setting and attainment produce results. The woman who sets high goals and achieves them inspires everyone who knows her.

The word "goal" provokes different emotions in people. Some people refuse to set goals for fear of failure. Some people don't have a vision; they live day to day never thinking that there may be more to this existence. Having goals gives us direction; they are our life's compass. Great athletes, entrepreneurs and high achievers use goal setting to accomplish their life's mission. Having goals helps you focus your attainment of knowledge and organize your resources. Goal setting gives you long-term vision and short-term motivation. Short-term goals are steppingstones to your long-term goals.

Discover what you want. What do you want out of your relationships, your career, your life? One way to discover your purpose, to create a vision for your life, is to make a detailed list of your hopes, dreams, and aspirations. Start by answering in detail the following questions:

1. What would you do if you won a million dollars today?

2. What makes you the happiest, most fulfilled?

3. What do you think about when you daydream?

4. What do you talk about most of the time?

5. If you were granted three wishes, what would they be?

6. What would you most like to achieve in the following areas of your life: career/business, health, family life, spiritually, education, community?

7. If you could travel anywhere in the world, where would you go and why?

8. What would you most like to be doing at this very minute? Where would you like to be?

9. What is most important to you: family, career, health, community, personal development, education, spiritual development, or enlightenment? The answer to this question will help you prioritize the list in question six.

10. What, if any, bad habits would you like to quit?

11. What possessions would you most like to have (new car, house, etc.)?

12. In what type of adventures would you like to participate most (racing, backpacking, skydiving, etc.)?

13. Whom would you most like to meet during your lifetime?

Discovering the answers to these questions will help you develop your life plan and categorize your goals list. You will be able to crystallize those things that are most important to you. To help you with this process, you can download the PMS™ Goals Discovery Chart at **http://www.speakingwithspirit.com/freearticles.asp.**

Plan

It takes as much energy to wish, as it does to plan.

– Eleanor Roosevelt

Create well-formed goal statements. In 1979, Harvard Business School did a study of its MBA graduates. They interviewed the graduates and asked them if they had clear written goals with plans for their careers when they left school. Only three percent had clear written goals with plans. Thirteen percent had goals, but they were not written down and did not necessarily have a plan. Eighty-four percent had no goals at all. Ten years later, Harvard did follow up interviews with the following results: the thirteen percent who had goals were earning on average twice as much as those with no goals at all. The most enlightening part was that the three percent who had written goals were earning on average ten times as much at the other ninety-seven percent put together!

What have you already done? Make a list of those goals you have accomplished already. No matter how small or insignificant they may seem, putting your accomplishments in writing motivates you. This exercise will fuel the fire to accomplish more goals.

Goals should be written in the affirmative and in the present tense. They should be well-defined and in as much detail as possible. When writing this chapter, my goal was to complete the first draft of my chapter in *Life Compass for Women*—in *one week*. Each author was allowed to write up to 2,500 words for her chapter. From past experience I knew I had to write at least 300 words a day in order to finish the chapter in a week. Did I do it? Yes. Some days I wrote 500 words and others I wrote 100 words, averaging 350 words per day, thereby accomplishing my goal on schedule. Because I am usually working on at least five major goals at once along with several short-term goals, it is necessary for me to put into writing a plan, prioritize my goals and work at each of them almost daily.

As a journalist, Rose Lee Archer knows the value of writing things down. Ever since she can remember she has been writing out her goals. Her goals are based upon how she sees her life. Her visions are generally "bigger than life." That requires a plan. She also knows that if she comes close, she has done a service to humanity and fulfilled her purpose. A teen mother of a disabled son, her vision was to create a venue to raise awareness of the value of hiring people with disabilities. The result was DADEO—Disability Awareness Disability Employment Opportunities. In October 2003 (Disability Employment Awareness Month) her vision was realized when she brought together dozens of resources in one location, touching thousands of people during a three day event. For her efforts and vision, *The South Florida Business Journal* honored Rose Lee Archer with the 2004 **diversityWORKS**! Award – Best Initiative in Human Interest.

In order to achieve your goals you must have self-discipline, focus and a burning desire to succeed—to do whatever it takes to get a job done. Take responsibility for your own actions and admit when you have made a mistake. It is important to be flexible and willing to change your course of action when necessary. Your goals must be specific and realistic, challenging yet attainable. If you set your expectations too high you will become frustrated and likely quit. Your goals should be measurable. If you want to write a book, you must pick up a pen and *write* at specifically scheduled times.

Prioritize your goals. The next step is to prioritize your list. Whether you have a list of 10, 20 or 100 goals, decide which ones are most important to you. Which goals would leave you feeling the happiest and most fulfilled? Number your goals, with *number one* being most important. Number one on your list would then be the goal on which you would focus the majority of your time, effort, and planning. Some of your goals will be simple to accomplish and yet give you a great sense of satisfaction. Be sure you make time to work on them as well.

Create an action plan. Once you know which goals you want to accomplish, develop an action plan—a manageable way to organize the tasks to achieve your goals. It should include the following:

- the goal
- the area of your life to which it pertains
- the deadline for accomplishing the goal
- the reasons you want to accomplish this goal
- possible obstacles that might stand in the way of accomplishing this goal

- solutions to the obstacles
- sacrifices/risks you will encounter
- what will inspire you to accomplish this goal
- list of people who could help you achieve your goals
- list of resources available/needed
- to-do list of prioritized tasks necessary to accomplish your goal
- how you will celebrate (reward yourself) once you accomplish your goal

This is an example of using the **PMS™** (**P**roductivity **M**anagement **S**ystem™) for Success in Goal Achievement. Filling in all the information listed above empowers you to succeed. Breaking down your goals down into manageable pieces reduces stress and makes the goals seem more attainable. If you would like to receive a downloadable version of the **P**roductivity **M**anagement **S**ystem™, you can request one at heidi@edenflorist.com.

Visualize your goals. Successful athletes visualize achieving their goals, winning the game, hitting the target.

Aimee Schmitt, former All-American swimmer at Stanford and author of *The Ultimate Swim Log & Goal Planner*, says, "One of my goals was to be able to visualize and go through a pre-race routine everyday… I focused on keeping my thoughts together and how I was going to do in the race, especially on what I was going to do the first 50 meters…" Her advice to fellow athletes was "to picture the race, where the opponents will be, what the crowd will sound like, the temperature and taste of the water, how the atmosphere will smell, the electricity of the moment, and what it will be like to touch the wall first. I guarantee you it will elevate your heart rate and blood pressure!"

You don't have to be an athlete to train like one—mentally that is. It is not enough to identify your goals. You must be able to *see* yourself achieving them. When you vividly imagine your goals as accomplished, your subconscious mind begins to recognize and attract all the resources you need to make your goal a reality. The more real your visualization, the more effectively this works. Once you visualize your success, you are that much closer to accomplishing your goals. Imagine what your life will be like once you accomplish your goals.

Manage

Everything worthwhile, everything of any value,
has a price. This price is effort.

– Loretta Young

Set reminders and deadlines. Schedule deadlines and reminders in the same way you schedule appointments and celebrations. Use your PDA, Day Planner, or calendar to list the deadlines and reminders.

Review your goal plan regularly. Perhaps the most important step in the goal management process is reviewing your goals. A common reason for failing to achieve goals is omitting the *review* step. Reviewing your goals keeps them fresh in your mind and keeps you motivated and focused on what is important. Review also allows you to make adjustments and change your goals when necessary. One of the best ways to review your goals is to look at your goals chart daily, see what steps you need to take and "do it!" Putting the goal in the forefront of your consciousness makes you think about it often. It helps you to better manage your time.

Remain flexible. Plan for flexibility and change. Be ready to change course when and if necessary in order to accomplish your goals.

Before she wrote her first book, Jonnetta "Coach" Chambers, M.A., thought about it for nearly ten years. Scheduled to speak at a women's business conference she mentioned to the event manager that she was writing a book. The program brochure announced her as Jonnetta Chambers, "Author of *Success Does Not Come on a Silver Platter* which will be available for sale during the event." That gave her just two months to finish the book and have it available for those participants who expected to buy it at the conference. And she did it. "Coach" Chambers is the founder of the Women in Focus Forum.

Succeed

*Success is about deciding what's important versus
what's irrelevant in your life; it's about self-motivation,
self-discovery, self-confidence and enjoying
the rewards of achieving your goals.*

– Heidi Richards

Associate with the right people. A great way to increase your chances
for success is to share your goals with others—those people who can give
you help and support your efforts. The very best advice I can give you is to
avoid negative people—those toxic people who bring you down. You know
the ones. For every positive thing you say, something negative comes out
of their mouths.

Persist until you succeed. If your goal is important to you, within
your reach and realistic, never give up. Some people give up just before
they achieve real success. Don't let that happen to you.

Randy Biro, Ph.D., always loved school. She remembers making
her brothers sit quietly while she played teacher as a child. At a
young age Randy knew she wanted to be a teacher and worked to
achieve her goal. After graduating from college she made a commitment to get her doctoral degree by the time she was 50 years
old. It was her gift to her parents for all of their support and the
many sacrifices they made so that she could achieve her goals.
Fourteen years after receiving her master's degree in Urban Education, she tackled her goal. She had no idea what she was getting
into or what sacrifices she would have to make when she enrolled
in the doctoral program. Working full time at a stressful, time-
consuming job, it took every spare moment she had to complete
her coursework. Much to the chagrin and patience of her very loving, supportive life partner, she gave up a very active social life.
Four and a half years later, her parents, boyfriend and best friend
watched as she proudly walked down the aisle, graduating with a
Doctoral Degree in Sociology of Education—the same month she
turned 50!

Be willing to sacrifice small things for the bigger, nobler accomplishments. Be patient. Incubation time is often necessary in order to attract the right events, resources and people to help you to achieve your goals.

Reward yourself. When you accomplish a goal, celebrate! Reward yourself in ways that make you feel good about your accomplishments. When you do, your subconscious recognizes the positive reinforcement and tells you that if you did it once, you can do it again.

It's Your Turn

What do you expect out of life? By now, you should be able to answer that question by using goal setting to *power* your life. Now you know the steps you need to achieve your goals. Using the PMS (Plan, Manage, and Succeed) formula outlined in this chapter, you can and will increase your opportunities for a more meaningful life. When you plan your goals, create and manage your plan of action, and visualize your success, you will do whatever it takes to become a master goal achiever! Dream big and believe that almost anything is within your reach. Because it is!

When I dream big, I see the possible, I discover potential,
and realize that almost anything is within my reach.
When I am willing to take a chance on me,
do whatever it takes, thank those who have helped me
along the way, and remember to pat myself on the back
once the goal has been reached, I am fulfilled.

– Heidi Richards

CHAPTER FIFTEEN

Cranial Aerobics for the Family
Generational bonding through play

Vicki Trembly

Vicki Trembly has another point of view! Comic, author and former talk show host, Vicki has a unique approach to dealing with the challenges everyone faces.

Did you know that the body contains 100 million sensory receptors to hear, see, taste, touch and smell in physical reality? The brain contains 10,000 billion synapses. So technically you are 100,000 times better equipped to experience an imaginary world than you are a real one. Cranial Aerobics is a high-energy workshop that exercises your mind and your sense of humor.

Vicki is a co-author of *Career Compass for Women* and a regular contributor to *HersKansas* magazine. She tours as a speaker and comic and performs regularly with Topeka Civic Theatre's improvisational company, Laughing Matters.

Her diverse background includes media salesman, talk show host, care-giver, promotions manager, copywriter, producer, water meter reader, Sunday School teacher, and master gardener.

Cranial Aerobics
Topeka, KS • 785-224-5408 • www.cranialaerobics.com

Vicki Trembly

Cranial Aerobics for the Family
Generational bonding through play

The family that plays together stays together. I typed that phrase into my search engine and in only .24 seconds I had more than 330,000 sites with those words in the title list. So it must be true. But a person can only stand so many trips to Candy Land. Playing is not just for kids anymore.

My mom used to say that babies were born with smooth brains and every time they saw something new, their brain got a wrinkle. It turns out my mama was right! Sort of.

Our brain cells start out smooth. As we grow and learn, these cells develop finger-like growths called dendrites that reach out to the other cells to facilitate communication and exchange information.

At a certain point as we age dendrite growth stops and we begin to lose brain cells. This contributes to dementia and Alzheimer's diseases. But new studies show that this deterioration can be stopped. Dr. Arnold B. Schiebel, a neurosurgeon and director of the Brain Research Institute at University of California at Los Angeles, claims that any activity that challenges your brain can stimulate the growth of dendrites.

So how do you grow a dendrite?

- Do things that are unfamiliar to your brain.
- Force your brain to think in a different direction.
- Make learning a lifetime habit.

The Cranial Aerobics exercises in this chapter are adapted for use with children as well as older relatives. Cranial Aerobics fosters communication between the generations and stimulates the kind of brain activity that slows the aging process—in a fun way.

These exercises grow connections not only from brain cell to brain cell but from generation to generation. By interacting in a playful way with older family members, children develop a sense of family history while older loved ones benefit from the mental stimulation of communicating, playing and laughing like a child.

Most of these games can be played anywhere. Feel free to adapt them to fit your family needs. In fact, please send me your suggestions at trainervik@cranialaerobics.com. I love learning new games.

There are four rules of Cranial Aerobics:

1. Pay attention.
   It sounds simple enough, but sometimes you worry so much about what you are going to say that you forget to pay attention to what is going on. When that occurs you lose valuable information. Absorb as much information as you can. Process the important stuff and file the rest.

2. Don't deny.
   Cranial Aerobics is play for the brain. Roy H. Williams wrote in *Accidental Magic* that the body contains 100 million sensory receptors to hear, see, taste, touch and smell in physical reality. The brain contains 10,000 *billion* synapses. So you're 100,000 times better equipped to experience an imaginary world than a real one. Anything can happen in your mind.

3. Take a risk.
   A Cranial Aerobics workshop is a safe, fun environment that encourages the oddest behavior. It is okay to laugh out loud or say something ridiculous.

The final and most important rule!

4. Have fun.
   Laughter is the greatest gift we have. It breaks down barriers and creates family bonds that last forever.

The goal of Cranial Aerobics is to make you laugh. If you're doing that, you're winning the game.

Celebrities

Two or more players
Equipment: You will need a timer of some kind. You can use a fancy electronic timer, stop watch, a timer purloined from another game, a small egg timer, or simply a watch with a second hand. You will also need a score pad and paper and pencils.

This game challenges your knowledge of famous celebrities. It is perfect for parties, scout meetings, Bible classes and family re-unions. Although you can play with two people, this game is more fun in larger groups. The more the merrier!

To start, each player writes the name of ten famous people on indi-vidual scraps of paper. You could choose a category, like Bible figures, actors, authors, presidents, politicians, historical figures, etc., or allow a combination for a wider variety. No matter what criteria you use for the famous names, I promise you will learn something every time you play.

Place all the names in a bowl and mix well. Decide on a length of time from 30 seconds up to one minute. Let your time frame and age of the participants decide how fast the game goes.

Pair up into teams. If there are an uneven number of players, it is okay for one team to have three players. They will just have to share guessing and clue giving. Each team consists of a clue giver and a guesser alternating roles each time it is their turn. Teams take turns trying to score as many right answers as they can in the time allotted. Play continues until all celebrities have been named.

The timekeeper gives the signal and the clue giver begins by draw-ing a name and giving clues to a teammate who must name the celebrity. It is okay if you pull a name that you put in. Your partner may or may not know them so there is no advantage.

Do not use any form of the person's name in the clue or use a "sounds like..." clue. For example if they had the name Andy Rooney, they could not say, "sounds like Mandy Boony." Nor could they say "this man's name is the word **and** with a **y** on it."

Instead they could say "This is the man on *60 Minutes* that always says, 'did'ja ever notice....'" or "He has big eyebrows."

The clue giver should continue to give clues until the guesser gets the name. As soon as that happens, draw another name and continue until time runs out. Go fast! If your partner isn't getting the name, or if you don't know who the celebrity is, use creativity to get your partner to say the name.

Maybe you pull out the name Ruth Buzzi and you have no idea that she was a comic on the television show Laugh-In who played an old lady with her hairnet on backwards and hit an old man with her purse.

Your clue could be, "This woman's first name is like the candy bar... Baby......" Hopefully your partner is a chocolate lover and will say Ruth.

Then you might say "her last name is what a bee says ... with the first syllable of the chorus of old MacDonald had a farm on the end of it." (Buzz E)

When time is up, count how many the first team guessed correctly and move on to the next team. If they were working on a name when the time ended but did not say it correctly, that name goes back in the bowl.

Please know that this will not be as easy as it reads on this page. Both players need to listen carefully while thinking fast. This is very difficult for some and is very entertaining for the observers. Some very odd clues will be used and you may learn more than you ever wanted to know about famous people.

Sentences

Two or more players
No equipment needed

This is a creative thinking game. It is deceptively simple and can be hysterically funny. It can also open the lines of communication in a non-threatening way. Keep it light and listen closely. You might learn more than new words.

My youngest daughter, who invented the game, explained it like this: "I'll give you a word and you make a sentence, then you tell me a word and I will make a sentence."

It is a fabulous way to teach younger children language skills. When my word was "to," I said, "Barb gave two tutus to Shelly, too." After we finished laughing about how silly that sounded and wondered to where Shelly would wear the two tutus, we talked about how some words sound the same but mean something different.

You will learn things, too! I was a little suspicious when my teenage daughter suggested we play on the way home from school one day. She usually isn't much for frivolous interaction with parental figures.

I gave her the word "address." Her sentence was, "I need a dress for the prom." I pointed out to her that that was not exactly the spelling of which I was thinking, but I couldn't deny it was still a good sentence. And I did learn something.

She then gave me the word "credit card," which is technically two words. But she was taking a risk. Again, I could not refuse to make my sentence. So, combining my highly trained Cranial Aerobics skills with my keen mother's intuition, I said, "My credit card is maxed out."

She didn't think that sentence was funny. Neither did her dad. But they both learned something.

There are many variations you can play to keep the game interesting.

- Only use words naming things you see from the window.
- On vacation you might use words relating to things you have seen and done.
- Could you make all the sentences questions?
- Make a rule that your sentences have to rhyme.
- Try having all the sentences build a story.

Yes And/ Yes But

Two or more players
No equipment needed

This is one of my favorite Cranial Aerobics exercises.
Yes and, you can play it almost anywhere.
Yes and, with almost anyone.
Yes and, it can help build the lines of communication.
Yes and, you can get new ideas.
Yes and, you can be silly.
Yes and, that will make you laugh.
Yes and, laughter is as good for your abdominals as are sit-ups.
Yes and, it's easy to play.
Yes and, is the name of the game.

Just start with a statement and let each player use his or her imagination to build a story—line by line—always starting with the phrase, "Yes and."

It's a great story generator. You can use it at family reunions, on vacations, or as a way to start the kids talking about what they did in school.

With elderly loved ones, start with a statement like "You grew up on a farm" to stimulate memory, or "You have a busy day today" to encourage conversation. This increases brain activity that may help fight Alzheimer's and dementia.

This game also has an alter ego.

Like YES AND, it begins with a declarative statement.
Yes but, it's different.
Yes but, it isn't a big change.
Yes but, it makes you think in another direction.
Yes but, that can be a good thing.
Yes but, it's harder to continue the story.
Yes but it's a favorite of my teenage daughter's.
Yes but, she thinks she is arguing with me.
Yes but, I know that it's only a game.

Letter Toss

One or more players
Equipment: Stuffed toy

Letter toss is like jogging for your brain. It helps you become more spontaneous. The object of the exercise is simple enough for even young children and is great for mental stimulation. Go through the alphabet and say a word for each letter. For example... Avocado – Break – Couple – Dog – Energy – Fine – Goat...

You can do it alone, before you get out of bed in the morning, or at a stoplight on your way to work. It also will help clear your head if you find yourself stuck in a rut.

I do institute the no umm's—the no hesitations clause—for this game. This means you have to say the first thing that comes into your head. Do not say umm or hesitate in any way. You know thousands of words. As long as the word starts with the right letter, say it. Hesitation is actually a sign of denial. Censoring your answers is a learned activity that adults adopt so we don't rudely blurt out what we really think. But for this game, let your brain out to play.

To play in a group you'll need an object that can be thrown. You may go in order around the circle, but randomly tossing a toy helps improve your listening skills and introduces the element of surprise so you can't plan ahead to your letter.

Player one begins by saying a word that starts with the letter 'A' and throws the toy to another player. That player must immediately say a word that starts with 'B' and throw the toy to someone else. Remember, go fast and no umm's. The point is to let your dendrites run wild.

As simple as this game is, the variations are endless.

- Make it a rule that the words cannot be related. For example, the words cannot all be names of cities like Abilene, Boston, Chicago, etc. You will find that your mind will start associating naturally so this can be difficult.

- Start in the middle of the alphabet.

- Specify that the words *have* to be related. Maybe they should all be men's names or office products or things you can eat.

This is my favorite variation.

- Allow any player to change the sequence by saying 'reverse' after their word. The players must then work the alphabet backwards until someone else says reverse again. You still have to go through all the letters, even backwards.

Random Sentences

One or more players
Equipment: Dictionary, paper and pencil

This game exercises your creativity and expands your vocabulary. Randomly select a word from your dictionary, read the definition if you don't know it, and write the word down on your paper. My randomly picked word is depict, which means to portray or describe in vivid detail. That's exactly what I will now do.

For each letter of the word you choose, think of another word. Do this fast. No hesitations. If you are playing with others, they can choose their own words or build on yours. It doesn't matter if the words are related or not. You may find you naturally think of related words but it doesn't matter either way.

For my words I used:

D – Dog
E – Earth
P – Pit
I – India
C – Cob
T – Tip

Now, use all those words make in a sentence. Don't worry if your sentence isn't logical or even physically possible. In fact, if you are playing with kids, the sillier the better. It should be grammatically correct.

My **dog Tip** dug a **pit** in the **earth** all the way to **India** and uncovered a **Cobb** salad.

If you don't have a dictionary or paper and pencil handy, or, if you are playing with younger kids, use smaller three- to five-letter words for the starter word to make it easier to keep track of the letters.

Deviated Dictionary

One or more players
Equipment: Dictionary, paper and pencil

This last game is educational, silly, and very creative. Deviated Dictionary expands your vocabulary and inspires creative thinking. Save the words you develop and use them as a secret family language.

Flip through a dictionary and choose a word at random. Read the word, spell it aloud and then read the definition. Use the word in a sentence. That's the educational part. Now create a new word by spelling it backwards. Say the new word aloud and define it.

One of our words was "inebriate." After some discussion my family decided "etairbeni" (inebriate backwards) is a noun meaning: a hat decorated with chocolate éclairs. Then we used it in a sentence. "I bought a new etairbeni for Easter and gained ten pounds."

They say laughter keeps you young. The average four-year-old laughs about 200 times a day while the average adult laughs only two times per day. Do you suppose that is why you hardly every see a four-year-old with grey hair and wrinkles? Laughter not only tightens your stomach muscles, it tightens your family bonds. I hope these Cranial Aerobics exercises made you laugh out loud. Play nice.

CHAPTER SIXTEEN

Listening to the Messages of Your Soul
Mastering the basics of balance

Lillian Zarzar, M.A.

Lillian Zarzar, M.A., transfers principles that enhance self-awareness and improve productivity in your personal and professional life. She is an author, international speaker, and consultant who transforms people.

Lillian is the founder and owner of MIND*SHIFT*ˢᵐ, a Columbus, Ohio, based international company devoted to assisting individuals and organizations to shift perceptions, enhance inspirations, and increase awareness. She is the author of *Apple-osophy: Slices of Apple-Inspired Wisdom* and contributing author to *Breakthrough Secrets to Live Your Dreams*, *Inspiring Breakthrough Secrets to Live Your Dreams*, and *Conversations on Success*.

Self-mastery is a critical component of Lillian's message. She relates well to the audience and personalizes the information in an easy-to-understand, yet profound manner. Her message has been heard in the United Kingdom, Australia, South Africa, New Zealand, Ireland, and Southeast Asia.

For over ten years Lillian has motivated and inspired her audiences to "get to the core" of who they are. She uses her theme of "apple-osophy" using the universal fruit, the apple, to help participants tap into a new way of *thinking beyond by going within* and shifting their lives.

Lillian Zarzar holds a Bachelor of Science in Journalism from Ohio University and a Master of Arts degree in Speech Communication from Bowling Green State University. She is an active member of the U. S. National Speakers Association.

MIND*SHIFT*
Columbus, OH • 614-486-5523 • www.mindshift1.com

Lillian Zarzar, M.A.

Listening to the Messages of Your Soul
Mastering the basics of balance

Keeping your balance while leading a purposeful life is a challenge! Have you ever noticed that you are not given more than you can handle? We seem to manage in spite of all that happens. Yet sometimes *you* give more than you can manage well and become resentful. How can you do all that you do and stay in balance? How do you minimize stress while looking for that balance?

Humans are remarkable. You have the ability to desire what you want in life, to determine the course you will take in achieving it, and to decide what your priorities are to keep you on purpose. You are in control and you choose the risk and make the commitment to your success. You are resilient and flexible. Self-discipline and self-mastery are critical components of your compass. This chapter provides you with seven concepts to help you connect to your inner power, maintain your balance, and create the life you would love to have.

Listen to the messages of your soul

Have you ever told yourself "I knew that was going to happen," or "I had a feeling something was going on?" Your soul speaks through the heart every day. Messages flow constantly because you never stop thinking. When you become consumed with the business of life, it is difficult to listen to your own thoughts. Distraction prevents us from the quiet time necessary for our growth, doesn't it?

Every day, take a few minutes and quiet your mind. Think about a comfortable and blissful place you love. If you love boating, see yourself floating on the lake relaxing. If you love hiking, find a lovely area on top of a mountain you climbed and breathe in the fresh air. If you love the beach, envision yourself reclining on the sand with the sun warming your skin. Wherever you go, be present with the place and the feeling you have. Then, breathe deeply from your diaphragm to balance the left and right hemispheres of your brain. The message to your brain is "calm down." As your brain waves subside slowly, thoughts begin to drift in. Be aware of your breathing; aware of the sounds you hear as they lull you to quietness. In the deep stillness of the mind are the answers to questions and decisions to consider.

As you listen to the messages that flow through your mind, take a few moments and jot down the information. Sometimes the message is simply an answer to something you were pondering. Sometimes the messages flow like the Niagara Falls with torrents of thoughts! Write down what you hear in a journal. You'll be amazed at how your mind sifts the data and how a pattern develops over time. You have access to the answers. To think beyond, you must go within.

Isolate what inspires you

Have you ever thought about what inspires you? Consider this: recall a day when you didn't know what day it was, when you didn't know what time it was, and at the end of the day you remarked, *"Wow, what a great day!"* Ask yourself what you were doing that made the day go so quickly. Were you at work? Were you volunteering for a project in your community? Were you spending time with your children? Ask yourself what activity you were involved in that you were able to have more energy at the end of the day than when you started.

Isolating those moments gives you an idea of what you enjoy the most and on what activities you would love to spend more time. The next question is how can you do more of what you love to do and get paid for it? What are you willing to do to live more of those moments you love? What are you willing to trade off to have what you deserve in your life? What dreams seem to surface consistently?

Sometimes dreaming about what you would love to have in your life seems daunting. Yet you dream every day. Your dreams don't leave you. They emerge regularly. You never have a dream you can't fulfill. There *is* a way if you are willing to do what it takes. When you know what inspires you, and you would love to have it, then you are unstoppable. Desiring something enough brings the energy to persevere to achieve it.

Think about what inspires you, what you dream about, and ask yourself what would be a first step toward achieving it. Simplify the process. Take one step only until you get your bearings. Confidence builds as you move forward. If, for example, you have thought about going back to school, then the first step would be to phone for information from the schools in the area to find out what is available to study. Step two would be to gather the information and read it! Step three is to check on financial programs for which you are eligible. Step four is to decide which school would give you the best opportunity based on your values. And so on.

Are you inspired to author a book? Then take a writing course, join a writer's guild, author an article, script poetry, or produce your work as a gift for friends. They would love for you to autograph it! In other words, take a step every day in the direction of your dreams. You are a work in progress. Every step in your evolution gets you closer to who you are and what is important to you. By isolating what inspires you, greater focus is achieved. Daily inspirations are the impetus for your success.

Take the risk of finding yourself

You are magnificent. How fortunate that you have *you*! In other words, no one can be you better than *you* can. You are the *you* chosen to live this life in the way only *you* can. Stop making comparisons to others. They are who they are and they couldn't possibly be you any more than you could be who they are. Yet how often have you wished you could be more like someone else?

Why not ask instead how you could be a better version of you? You are the star of your production. Shakespeare reminded us that the entire world is a stage and we are players on it; you have your unique place, and each role you play is a dimension of you. Memorize your lines and learn your roles as you star in the movie of your life. And if you don't know your lines, write them!

Finding yourself opens the doors to the direction your life will take. What is your personality? Do you love being with people? Do you like numbers? Do you prefer to be in charge of projects? Do you like the limelight? Do you enjoy working in the background supporting others? So many questions—so many answers—only one you. Think about how you would love to spend your time and who you actually are.

Every day you are evolving. Ask yourself the deeper questions as you look inside yourself. Every day ask yourself what you are to do. Ask for guidance. You'll find that a magnificent person resides inside waiting to be discovered. You are worth exploring. The risk is minimal compared to the incredible being you'll uncover.

Every opportunity presents us with lessons in who we are and where we are going. As you find out who you are, as you uncover what brings you joy and sustenance, you learn to love yourself. Remember, love yourself for *who* you are rather than for whom you *think* you should be. Love yourself where you *are* rather than where you *think* you should be and you'll appreciate yourself that much more. Your journey to self-discovery is unique to you. Thus as you find yourself, the more you love yourself. The risk helps you dare to be you!

Identify your lopsided perceptions

Would you agree we see the world as we are because of our perceptions? Have you ever had something "bad" happen only to find that it was a "good" thing that it happened? You also may have experienced a crisis to find the hidden blessing in the situation.

Stress is greater when you view a situation from only one side and think that it is the only side to see. Remember that there are always two sides to everything. A way to stay in balance is to look for both sides of the issue.

For example, an optimist sees a glass of water as half-full, and the pessimist sees it as half-empty. Actually, *it can't be half-full unless it is also half-empty!* One side cannot exist unless the other is present. Because of our lopsided perceptions, we see the side comfortable for us at that moment. When you observe someone being nasty, remember they have a nice side they are not showing you at the moment.

Opposites come from each other. You know where west is because you know east; you know what is in from what is out, down from up, north from south, and so on. When you feel something is a benefit, look for the drawback. When you see the drawback, find the benefit. Human emotion is the same. While you are expressing sadness, you are repressing happiness and vice versa.

Wisdom is being able to see the two sides and be grateful. Both are necessary for understanding, both have value, and both are there even if you don't realize it. When you see the world as it is, you recognize the value of each side and your emotions remain in check to minimize stress and maximize balance.

Learn the balance of the universe

You are a part of a magnificent universe. You are made of the same elements as the rest of the world. Everything pulsates with its own energy frequency. Energy fluctuates and we are part of the ebb and flow of the energy fields. You transmit and receive electromagnetic impulses from the world around you. That is why we say someone is on the same "wavelength" or it is "chemistry" between two individuals.

In the grander scheme, the world is constantly in balance through the electromagnetic impulses transmitted and received. Therefore you will be supported and challenged in every situation simultaneously. You experience both positive and negative elements *throughout* your life, just as you express both the positive and negative *in* your life. The balance of the universe is always there, even though you may not be aware of it.

Since you are part of the divine design of the world, you have a purposeful place. You belong here within the balance of the universal order and structure. The Creator makes no mistakes. All happens for a reason and all happens in the fullness of its time. All is purposeful and all is mindful. The brilliance of our existence is that we *do* exist. You have the ability to create the masterpiece of your life by understanding that all that exists is already in balance. Thus, as you realign your perspective and realize your existence is part of a divine order, an opportunity that appears difficult is the one that helps you grow and appreciate your part in the world.

Within your energy field in the world, your direction comes from your choices. Your choices come from your decisions. Your decisions come from the questions you ask of yourself. By asking questions of various frequencies or levels of energy, the quality of your life is affected. For example, if you ask the time, anyone can tell you. Or, if you ask "How can I make it to the end of the week?" then that is the answer you receive and you will just "make it" to the end of the week. Thus, questions of a lower frequency are easiest to answer. They emanate from a different wavelength.

If, however, you ask questions of a higher frequency, they elevate your existence to a higher purpose. For example, you may ask, "How can I mobilize the resources of my life to have what I love?" or "What can I do to make a difference in someone's life?" Since the divine order provides you the chance to create your life, then purposeful questions bring a higher value to your life.

In the bigger picture of the world, your life takes on a new meaning. As you appreciate that the world is in balance, finding your own balance becomes apparent. Ask yourself higher-level questions daily, because as you tap into the balanced energy of the universe, you will become more balanced yourself. Your course is charted optimally when you mobilize your energy at the highest frequency of the universe. The more you are aware of the universal balance, the more balance you have in your immediate world.

Live life in appreciation and grace

Gratitude is the wellspring of inspiration. Recognizing that all has purpose and meaning brings comfort. Whatever you do you will be supported, challenged, and loved in the process.

One of the most inspiring exercises is to be grateful for all that is in your life whether you consider it to be positive or negative. Everything in the universe serves, or it would not exist. Start each morning with an exercise of appreciation and you will find that you embrace the day with greater love and understanding.

As you breathe deeply and still the noise in your brain, begin your gratitude exercise. Think about everyone who has helped you throughout your life. Think about those who were there for you when you needed support. Think about your family, thanking each member for being in your life. Think about those who challenged you to live up to your values. They, too, are great teachers on your journey to balance and wholeness.

Think of the events that brought both sorrow and happiness and be grateful. Think of the world events that seem unfair or unjust and be grateful. Think of the people who are kind and mean and be grateful. They all serve a purpose; they are all part of your journey to loving yourself. Because you are reflected in them as they are in you.

Finding a few minutes each day to be in a state of grace brings inspiration and power to your life. Throughout the day, notice as you may drift from your purpose and bring yourself back to being present in the moment. Presence and patience balances us. Accepting and appreciating all that is as it is brings calmness and bliss.

Remind yourself every day how deserving you are.

Apply what you know

What you know and what you do are two different processes.

Identify your values. Take the time to list what values are functioning in your life. Ask yourself what you believe. Those values and beliefs are the underpinnings of your behavior. They drive your existence and move your spirit. Watch yourself through the day and think about what you do and why you do it.

Look for what inspires you. Take time to center yourself every day to bring greater appreciation for your life. Evaluate the moments most significant to you. Be realistic of what you can express and expect. Make the most of those inspiring times. Obtain a blank book and journal your thoughts daily.

Take the risk to connect with yourself. Get to know and love yourself. Spend time with yourself. To be afraid to be alone is to be afraid to take risks. The biggest risk is taking none.

Carve out specific time for yourself. Make a date or have a meeting with yourself to reflect on why you are who you are and who you are becoming.

Recognize that all is purposeful. Everything in the world has a purpose and a service to you and to others. Ask what *your* service is. Take advantage of opportunities that present themselves to you. Jump in and see what happens! If you make a mistake, you have learned. Therefore you benefit from the situation.

Appreciate the balance of the universe. Realize that you are part of the divine design of life. Live your life significantly. Imagine all those who will be deprived of your wisdom if you don't share it. Be grateful for even the difficult people in your life who serve as teachers of the lessons you are learning.

Enjoy the daily rituals of life; becoming a fully integrated and healthy human is a process. Commit each day to becoming your best. You are worth it. Make the choice each day as to how you will embrace the day. Decide what is most important and live with purpose and conviction. Your thoughts about yourself are the driving force of your success. If you think you can, you can!

You know much more than you use. The concepts here are not new to you. You have heard some of them before in other words or other frameworks. Use what you know! Start with one of the ideas and focus on mastering that concept. You are important enough to become the master of your life. Taking a few minutes every day for *you* is a good place to start.

Create the life you deserve and be humble to the messages of your soul. Your soul speaks through the heart and the heart knows the truth. Listen. Follow. Your life is a journey—enjoy it!

Life Compass for Women

The Indispensable Guidebook on Life
Management for Busy Women

Additional Resources From
Karen L. Anderson

Workbook:

Living Letters: How to Make a GREAT Relationship – $22 including S/H

Books:

The Busy Manager's Guide to Successful Meetings
Proof Positive: How to Find Errors Before They Embarrass You
Magnetic Leadership

Adult Learning Programs:

Adult Learning Methods

Persuasive Presentations

E-mail Professionalism & Composition

Professional Writing Program

Grant Writing Strategies

Grammar, Punctuation, Usage & Proofreading

How to Stay in Control in the Midst of Chaos

Customer Service: You ARE the Organization

Super Supervisory Skills for Non-profits

Empowerment and Forgiveness

Professional Protocol and Presence

Life's Lessons in Your Hands

(Other titles and topics upon request.)

ORDERING INFORMATION

Anderson Catalyst Training Services
7923 Noland Road, Lenexa, KS 66215-2528
Office: 913-492-3881/1-800-414-3881, code 44
Fax: 913-492-5054
www.acts-ion.com
Email: Karen@acts-ion.com

Speeches, Seminars & Booklets:

- Africa to America / Cultural Diversity – When Worlds Meet
- Change Management – When Certainty Crumbles
- Conflict Resolution – Good Fences Make Good Neighbors
- Creative Image – Visible Original or Invisible Photostat
- Global Competitiveness – Nature Hates a Vacuum
- Leadership for Geniuses – Remaining King of the Jungle
- Meeting Excellence – Boardroom or Bored Room
- Modern & Future Life – Just Add Water
- Motivation & Morale – Why the Chicken Crossed the Road
- Performance & Nonperformance – Zero Defect & Murphy's Law
- Personal Professional Mastery – You Don't Have to Be Sick to Get Better
- Scenario Planning – Prophetic & Profitable Solutions
- Team Players of Tomorrow – Wholistic Me & We
- Time Warp Management – On the Edge of the Speed of Dark
- Values & Ethics – Risking the Rules

CONTACT INFORMATION

Larna Anderson Beebe
Overland Park, KS
913-642-1114
www.responsegroup.com/larna
Email: andersonbeebe@sbcglobal.net

Additional Resources From Darla Arni

Educational Materials:

Sharing Creative Energy E-newsletter – Subscribe online and view past issues
30 Ways to Share Creative Energy at Home! – booklet

Presentations and Programs:

- The Creative Mindset
- Creativity Killers
- Creating Time & Balance
- Playing with a Purpose Teambuilding & Corporate Games

CONTACT INFORMATION

Sharing Creative Energy
Darla Arni
529 Rich
Slater, MO 65349
660-529-2969
www.darlaarni.com
darlaarni@socket.net

Additional Resources From Allison Blankenship

Complimentary Articles through www.AllisonSpeaks.com:

"Simple Signals that Sabotage Clear Communications"
"It's EASY to Say No"
"How to Be Assertive without Being Pushy"
"A+A=S Formula for Success"
"Say Yes to You!"

Educational Materials:

Mission Possible IV

Allison joins noted authors and speakers Jack Canfield, *Chicken Soup for the Soul*, and Brian Tracy, *The Psychology of Achievement*, in a collection of strategies on becoming more successful. This engaging, easy-to-read format includes ideas from artists to athletes to entrepreneurs. $15; available through www.AllisonSpeaks.com.

Stress-less Life Solutions online-coaching

A 27-day email course designed to create a more balanced and fulfilling life. Each daily issue coaches you through key areas such as getting over guilt, finding time to replenish your soul, easy ways to say "no" and free up your schedule, managing your personal energy, plus finding creative quality time with your loved ones. $27; available through www.AllisonSpeaks.com.

Keynotes and Workshops:

NEW! *Life Divas: A Woman's Journey* – entertaining, inspiring three-woman show on living an authentic and fulfilling life
Real Women Have Chipped Nails – life balance and self-management strategies
Flat Cats Don't Fly – make conflict comfortable and productive
Communicating with Tact and Finesse – what to say in difficult situations
SpeakEasy – persuasive and powerful presentation skills
How to Be Assertive without Being Pushy – get results with respect

Gift Ideas:

'Queen of the Universe' T-shirt: $15
Tiaras: $4-10

ORDERING INFORMATION

Allison Blankenship
Life's Simple Solutions, Inc.
800-664-7641
www.AllisonSpeaks.com

Services:

Human Resource Training
Conference, Key Note, or Dinner Speeches
Facilitation of Team Meetings or Planning Retreats
Planning & Conducting Focus Group Sessions
Individual Coaching for Managers/Supervisors
Assistance in Development of In-house Training Programs

Training Topics:

- Team Building Behaviors
- Communications Styles
- Problem Solving Techniques
- Customer Service Excellence
- Innovation / Creative Thinking
- Business Ethics for Today
- Stress, Time & Conflict
- Developing Leadership Skills
- Pathways to Positive Relationships
- Navigating Difficult Conversations
- Empowerment Strategies
- Humor in the Workplace
- BEST Supervisory Techniques
- Behavioral Interviewing
- Effective Performance Reviews
- Coaching for Success
- Process Improvement
- Discipline Issues
- The Fish Philosophy

CONTACT INFORMATION

A Place in Time
PO Box 87
Tecumseh, KS 66542
www.tonisplace.com
training@tonisplace.com
785-379-8463

Additional Resources From Ann Mah

Get reprints of Ann's articles from *HersKansas* magazine to grow your business skills. Over twenty articles available including:

"Mentoring Teamwork" – Identifying a mentor can be the missing link when you're trying to make connections or find a friendly ear.

"Work Past 'No'" – Women don't have to be on the wrong side of the negotiating table. Play up your bartering strengths.

"30 Seconds" – Does your personal style open doors for your career, or is the door getting slammed in your face? Discover the secrets of making waves.

"Casual or Casualty?" Don't dress down your career aspirations. Dress the part.

"Let's Do Lunch" Follow the rules when dining out to get ahead in your career.

"Can You Hear Me Now?" Be sure you are getting your message across.

"Find the Leader in You" Think credibility, vision and communication when stretching your skills.

"Lower Your Center of Gravity" Seize control of your schedule to maintain balance in your life.

"Go With the Flow" Change is inevitable, but you can make it easier on yourself.

"When Bad Behavior Happen to Good People" Strategies for dealing with conflict in the workplace.

"Career Connection" How to turn your boss into an ally.

Price: $2.00 each or a set of 12 for $15.00.

CONTACT INFORMATION

Ann E. Mah – Discover! Strategies
Office: (785) 266-9434
Website: www.annmah.com
Email: ann@annmah.com

Additional Resources From Susan Meyer-Miller

Videos:

Step Up and Lead – Four part video series

Step Up and Lead features Susan Meyer-Miller, award-winning international speaker and trainer. Our corporate training videos focus on leadership skills, leadership image, mastering motivation, mediating employee conflicts, employee development and performance. Only $99.00 plus shipping and handling for all four videos.

Set includes:
Video 1: Establishing Yourself as a Leader (1 hr 45 min)
Video 2: Creating Synergy Through People Skills (1hr)
Video 3: The Leader as Coach: How to Bring Out the Best in Individual Team Members (1 hr 45 min)
Video 4: Solving Performance Problems (45 min)
Also available individually for $29.95 plus shipping and handling.

Books:

SOS! 101 Solutions to Overcome Stress is our book filled with practical and humorous solutions for getting through stressful situations.
Available for $6.95 + S&H

Speak with Power Passion and Pizzaz – 333 tips to delight your audience. By Susan Meyer- Miller and Dr. Prasad Kodukula. $16.95 + S&H

Career Compass for Women – The Indispensable Guidebook for Women in the Workplace. 14 mini-workshops in a book with practical career advice. Co-authored by Susan Meyer-Miller.

ORDERING INFORMATION

SpeakerUSA
Susan Meyer-Miller
Shawnee, KS
1-877-674-8446
(913) 248-1485
www.SpeakerUSA.com

Additional Resources From
Connie Michaelis

Most Frequently Requested Programs:

- Image: Inside and Out
- "More Than A Pink Cadillac"
- Personal Packaging: You Are Your Product
- Personal Growth: Spiritual, Emotional, Financial
- Living On Purpose
- Finding Your Purpose, Passion and Plan
- Professional Image Seminars
- Personal Motivation Seminars
- Seasonal Trend Report From Milan, Paris and New York
- How to Look Like a Million for $9.95!

CONTACT INFORMATION

Connie Michaelis
785-271-6804
Email: mkconnie@cox.net
www.marykay.com/conniem

Most Requested Live Programs:

Training

Servant Leadership: Building Leadership Excellence
Character and Building Team Work Excellence
Diversity Competence in the Workplace

Keynotes

Five Sacred Principles to Living Life with Serenity, Satisfaction, and Joy
Bringing Out the Greatness in You
Middle Age: It's the Sweet Center of Life

CONTACT INFORMATION

Debra Neal
Pathways to Empowerment
Office: 816-805-0732
Email: dneal@everestkc.net
www.pathwaystoempowerment.net

Additional Resources From Jae Pierce-Baba

Books:

Fantastic Customer Service: Inside and Out
Jae's chapter: *Pardon Me Dear... I Believe You May Have Forgotten Which Side Of The Counter You Are On.*
This book is a compilation of expert coaching advice and a great addition to every organization's library. Enjoy the inspirational and entertaining selection of case studies written by a variety of experts in customer service, including Jae!

Putting the Ahh-Ha! Back into Teaching and Parenting
This book is full of information that combines sensory integrative techniques and educational principals to encourage children to be as successful as possible. Written in a humorous style with colorful graphics.

Most Requested Live Programs:

- Motivation is an inside job: Renewal, Rejuvenation, and Restoring Oneself Through The Power Of Laughter (Health and healing)
- Today is the First Day of the BEST of your life (keynote)
- One Laugh is Worth A Thousand Nags (parenting)
- Don't Complain About The Coffee: You May Be Old and Weak Yourself Someday! (aging)
- Preventing Hardening of the Attitudes in the Golden Years (geriatrics/aging parents)
- Mirth in Management: The Bottom Line and The Punch Line Do Intersect! The Power of Humor in Business (corporate/customer service)
- Dealing With Challenging Situations, Difficult People and Annoying Co-Workers

ORDERING INFORMATION

Jae Pierce-Baba – LipShtick Productions
12206 Ridgepoint
Wichita, Kansas 67235
Office: 316-946-0422
Fax: 316-946-0840
Web: www.jaepierce-baba.com
Email: jae@jaepierce-baba.com

Additional Resources From Heidi Richards

Books:

Self-Marketing Manual $67.00

A comprehensive marketing manual filled with "how to" ideas to market your business, create a publicity frenzy, and become a "celebrity" in your community and your industry. Comes with the Self-Marketing Dictionary, complete with dozens of forms you can modify to fit your own needs (Your choice of floppy disc or CD.)

The PMS Principles: Powerful Marketing Strategies to Grow Your Business $19.95

Whether you begin with networking, partnering, speaking, word-of-mouth or the dozens of other strategies to create your marketing plan, the PMS™ Principles delivers on its promise … to GROW your business; and you will do this without spending all your hard-earned cash.

Rose Marketing on a Daisy Budget – How to Grow Your Business Without Spending a Fortune $19.95

Jam-packed full of easy-to-do marketing ideas, valuable insights, real life success stories and resources to get the reader to create her own low-cost marketing campaigns today.

What's Your OccuPLAYtion? For Teachers $7.95

Filled with 149 ideas, motivational quotes and vignettes to increase job satisfaction, reduce stress, and get more joy out of your work and your life working in the hectic, sometimes unappreciated world of education.

What's Your OccuPLAYtion? For Nurses $7.95

Filled with 149 ideas, motivational quotes and vignettes to increase job satisfaction, reduce stress, and get more joy out of your work and your life in the hectic world of the health-care professional.

"Yes" Is Only The Beginning – 2ND Edition $5.95

The Ideal Wedding Planner – Traditions, Etiquette, and Checklists to Help You Plan the Perfect Wedding.

ORDERING INFORMATION

Heidi Richards
800-466-3336
www.heidirichards.com

Cranial Aerobics workshops
are available on a variety of topics including:

Spot Training for Media and Sales Professionals
Meeting-er-size – 20 minutes to a more effective meeting
Nuclear Networking – Making friends like a big kid
Recess for Grown-ups – Powerful Play for Professional Progress
Broga – Yoga for the Brain

A featured comic in *She's So Funny*, Vicki can emcee, feature or headline.
Vicki is also available for special events: birthdays, family reunions, etc. Make your next event something everyone will remember.

Books:

Career Compass for Women $14.95

Multiple Authors
Fourteen mini-workshops designed to point your career in the right direction.

She's so Funny $10.95

Edited by Judy Brown
A collection of over 1700 jokes by the country's funniest female comics.

Copies of past *HersKansas* articles are available for $2.00 each.
Titles are on the website www.cranialaerobics.com or contact Vicki Trembly at trainervik@cranialaerobics.com for titles and topics.

ORDERING INFORMATION

Contact Vicki Trembly
trainervik@cranialaerobics.com
785-224-5408
www.cranialaerobics.com

Additional Resources From Lillian Zarzar

Books:

Apple-osophy – Slices of Apple-Inspired Wisdom	$ 9.95
Breakthrough Secrets to Live Your Dreams	$19.95
Inspiring Breakthrough Secrets to Live Your Dreams	$19.95
Conversations on Success	$19.95

Presentation Topic Areas:

Spiritual Awakening
Tapping Inner Wisdom
Interpersonal Skills
Communication Techniques
Relationship Building
Understanding Conflict

CONTACT INFORMATION

Lillian Zarzar
MIND*SHIFT*
P. O. Box 21937
Columbus, OH 43221
614-486-5523
614-486-8119 (fax)
www.mindshift1.com

NOTES

NOTES

NOTES

NOTES